Standard Grade

History
revision notes

Text copyright © 1994 Alan J. Wilson
Design and layout copyright © 1994 Leckie & Leckie ltd

ISBN 0-9515718-9-3

Published by
Leckie & Leckie ltd, 8 Whitehill Terrace, St. Andrews, Scotland, KY16 8RN
tel. 01334 475656   fax. 01334 477392
enquiries@leckieandleckie.co.uk   www.leckieandleckie.co.uk

Edited by Des Brogan

Designed by Caleb Rutherford and Julie Barclay

Special thanks to Historic Scotland for permission to use the cover image.

A CIP Catalogue record for this book is available from the British Library.

Leckie & Leckie is a division of Granada Learning Limited, part of ITV plc.

These Notes cover the most popular Contexts of the Standard Grade History Course (*see over*).

It is impossible to cover absolutely everything but you will find that all the main topics are covered. Select only those chapters which you have studied in your History class and work your way carefully through the Notes. Care and concentration on each Context will help you achieve good results in your examination.

✕ Alan J Wilson ✕

DORNOCH ACADEMY

909
TNF

Contents

1. Changing Life in Scotland and Britain: Population 1750s – Present Day

1. Population growth

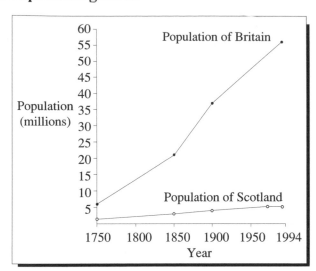

In 1750 the total population of Britain was about 6 million and the population of Scotland was about 1.25 million. Today the population of Britain is over 55 million and the population of Scotland is 5.1 million.

Recently, however, Scotland's population has been falling: 100,000 fewer people live in Scotland today than in 1971.

2. Reasons for population growth

- The Irish Famine of the 1840s caused mass emigration from Ireland to Britain.

- Medical improvements, especially after 1850, helped reduce the death rate.

- People were marrying younger and having larger families.

- More children survived their first five years of life.

- Better housing, improved water supply and better hygiene helped to stop the spread of disease in the second half of the 19th century.

- People were living longer because farming improvements provided a healthier diet.

3. Population movement

In 1750, 80% of the British population lived in the countryside. Today only 20% live in the countryside (and only 2.5% are employed in agriculture).

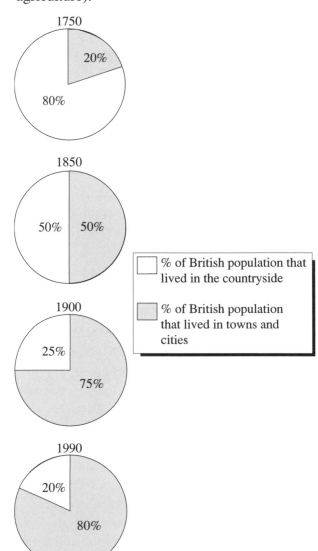

4. Reasons for population movement

A steady flow of people left the countryside because

- the increase in population meant more people were looking for jobs – these jobs were in the towns;

- new farming methods meant fewer people were needed to work on the land;

- enclosures resulted in families being forced to leave the countryside;

- poverty and eviction forced hundreds of Scots to leave the Highlands.

page learnt

5. Highland Clearances: cause and effect

Many people left the Highlands between 1800 and 1850.

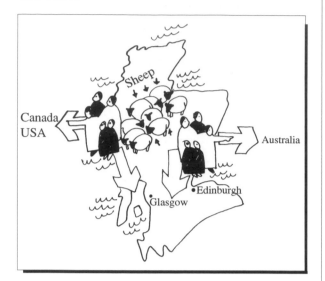

The introduction of sheep to the Highlands brought increased income to landlords. Landlords made a higher income from sheep farming than from tenanted farms.

Sheep needed large areas of land to graze on. Tenants were forced to leave their farms. Some crofters were moved to the coast. Some moved south to the growing towns and cities. Others emigrated overseas.

In spite of the Clearances, however, the population of the Highlands increased from 200,000 in 1750 to 300,000 in 1840.

6. Emigration from Scotland

Two million people left Britain and Ireland between 1815 and 1850. Most of the 100,000 who left Scotland emigrated to Canada, Australia and the USA. Many emigrants were promised free passage, cheap land and work for all.

Between 1895 and 1939, 1.4 million emigrated from Scotland, mostly to Canada and the USA. This high rate of emigration slowed down dramatically after 1929, when the Depression affected the countries which had previously welcomed immigrants.

7. Immigration to Scotland

Large numbers of people also came to live in Scotland between 1880 and 1939.

Many Irish came to Scotland to escape the Irish Famine which had caused widespread starvation and poverty. One quarter of Glasgow's population in the 1841 census was Irish. They became navvies and seasonal farm workers. There were many violent incidents, especially in and around Glasgow, because many were Roman Catholic and were seen to be taking precious jobs and houses.

- In 1881 there were over 200,000 Irish-born people living in Scotland.
- In 1911 there were almost 25,000 foreigners living in Scotland.
- In 1931 there were over 150,000 English- and Welsh-born people living in Scotland.

Between 1880 and 1939, almost 4 out of every 5 immigrants were Scots who were returning to Scotland.

2. Changing Life in Scotland and Britain: 1750s – 1850s

Technological change in agriculture

1. Out of date

By 1750 farming methods were out of date and unable to feed the growing population. In Scotland people lived in *ferm touns* surrounded by *infield* and *outfield* farmland. *Infield* farmland was situated near the centre of the farm. *Outfield* farmland was poorer land at the outskirts of the farm. Farmers grew their crops on *runrigs*. Animals grazed on common land.

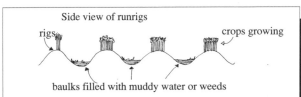

Side view of runrigs

rigs — crops growing

baulks filled with muddy water or weeds

Baulks were spaces between rigs which the farmers walked along to look after the crops. They often filled up with weeds which then grew onto the rigs killing the plants.

2. Improvements

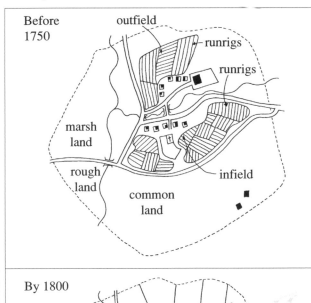

Before 1750

outfield
runrigs
runrigs
marsh land
rough land
infield
common land

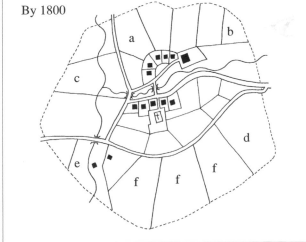

By 1800

a
b
c
d
e
f f f

2. Improvements (cont.)

Improvements in crop growing and animal rearing were already under way in England by 1750. Many Scottish landowners began to introduce better methods in Scotland. The introduction of improvements, however, was slow and uneven throughout the countryside.

- rigs replaced by enclosed fields which increased the amount of land under cultivation. The spaces between the rigs wasted good growing land. *See (a) in diagram.*

- fields surrounded by walls or hedges. These separated one farmer's field from another's. *(b)*

- marsh land drained *(c)*

- common land turned into fields *(d)*

- rough land cultivated *(e)*

- fertilisers – dung, lime and kelp – used in much greater quantities to improve the quality of the soil *(f)*

- new crops introduced to put nutrients back into the soil and to provide winter fodder for animals

- crop rotation introduced so that all fields could be used every year

- selective breeding improved the quality of livestock

- seed drills and threshing machines used in the 1780s; steam engines used after 1830

- long leases given to tenants to encourage improvements

3. Effects of improvements

- Many tenants could not afford to pay the higher rents demanded by landlords.

- Those who could not pay left the land and moved to the towns or became landless labourers.

- Many labourers were put out of work as new machinery was used on improved farms.

- Most improving landowners and the remaining tenant farmers had become very wealthy by 1850.

- More milk, dairy produce and fresh meat was available all year round. This improved the diet of those who could afford these foods. These people lived longer and had healthier children.

page learnt

Technological change in the textile industry

1. Out of date

By 1750 the cottage industries of spinning and weaving were out of date and unable to clothe the growing population. Textile inventions helped to replace the domestic system with the factory system of manufacture. The first purpose-built Scottish cotton mill opened in 1778.

2. Changes

- New textile machines began to be used on a large scale.
- Textile inventions became too large for farmers' homes, so factories were built to house them.
- Muscle and water power were replaced by steam power after 1781 with James Watt's invention of the steam engine.

Year	Spinning	Weaving	Power
1733		Kay's Flying Shuttle	Muscle
1763	Hargreaves' Spinning Jenny		Muscle
1769	Arkwright's Water Frame		Water
1779	Crompton's Mule		Water
(1781		James Watt's Steam Engine	Steam)
1785		Cartwright's Power Loom	Steam

3. Effects of the changes

- Cotton replaced wool as the most common material spun and woven in Britain.

Year	Raw cotton imported into Scotland
1775	0.14 million lbs
1812	11.00 million lbs

- The new factories needed huge workforces which were supplied by those who left the countryside.
- Goods could be made cheaply and in vast quantities. Manufactured cotton goods made up half Britain's exports by 1850.
- While work and wages were regular, hours were long, pay was low and conditions were poor.
- Child labour grew in an uncontrolled way until 1833. Children were cheaper to employ than adults.
- Many villages and towns, e.g. Paisley, New Lanark and Glasgow, grew in size, especially after the invention of the steam engine.
- 38% of Glasgow's population worked in textile mills by 1841.

Health and housing in the towns

1. Population movement

In 1750 only 20% of the population lived in towns; by 1850, 50% lived in towns. *(See page 3.)* Thousands of people poured into the towns in search of work. This rapid change had a great effect on the health and housing of the population.

At first many continued to live far from their work. By the early 1800s, however, factory owners and the workers themselves wanted workers' homes to be closer to the factories and mills.

2. Problems and diseases

Problems	Results
Need for houses	Rows of tenements built
Workers were unskilled and poor	Workers rented single-roomed flats
Workers had large families	Overcrowding
More people moved to towns	More cheap housing was built
Landlords failed to maintain houses	Growth of slums

The failure to tackle these problems properly led to poor living conditions and the spread of disease.

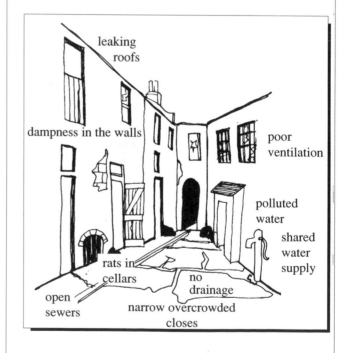

2. Problems and diseases (cont.)

Conditions	Diseases caused
Narrow overcrowded closes	Tuberculosis (TB) and typhus
Poor ventilation	Chest diseases (e.g. bronchitis) and TB
Open sewers and middens	Typhus
No drainage	Cholera
Flooded sewers and stagnant cesspools, no indoor toilets or running water	Cholera
Dampness in the walls	Chest diseases
Filth in the stairs	Typhus, Diphtheria
Polluted water from communal wells	Cholera
Rats, flies and lice everywhere	Typhus and typhoid
Several people sleeping in one room	TB
Communal toilets	Cholera
Poor diet	TB

The killer disease of the 1830s was **cholera**. 50% of all those who caught the disease died. It killed 10,000 in Scotland in 1831–2. Even by 1850 doctors still had little idea what caused it.

Health and housing in the countryside

1. Poor conditions

As enclosures began to take effect, most agricultural workers became farm labourers. Their housing conditions were very bad. Most workers lived close to poverty throughout their lives. Their diet consisted of broth, bread and vegetables. Their situation became even worse when crops failed.

Improvements brought wealth to landowners and tenant farmers. Their housing improved during the period.

However, poorer tenants who were unable to pay the increased rents demanded by improving landlords had to sell up their household possessions and leave or become landless labourers.

Hired labourers received a tied cottage and usually a small plot of land. Low wages meant only small cottages could be rented. Half of the cottage was shared with the labourer's animals.

1. Poor conditions (cont.)

Families were large, so overcrowding was as big a problem in the countryside as it was in the towns.

2. Poor health

Usually there was a much lower chance of disease in the countryside since the conditions there were not as overcrowded and filthy as in the towns.

However, when diseases, e.g. cholera, did affect the water supply of small villages, the percentage of deaths from diseases could be higher than in cities. Also, back-breaking work in all weathers contributed to a low standard of health and premature death.

Changes in working conditions on the land

Working conditions of British farmers changed slowly between 1750 and 1850.

While enclosures did force many off the land and turned many small farmers into landless wage labourers, this did not happen everywhere. It was only in areas where beef and sheep were profitable that the number of jobs in agriculture declined: 700,000 people were employed in agriculture in 1802; 760,000 people were employed in 1831.

Before improvements	After improvements
Farmers lived in *ferm touns*.	Individual houses were built near farmers' fields.
Farmers worked in groups.	Tenant farmers hired labourers.
One-third of the rigs were unused each year. Some only grazed animals on common land.	All fields were used each year by crop rotation. They lost everything.
Farmers were given short leases.	Farmers were given long leases.
Animals were killed before winter.	Animals were foddered over winter.
Seeds were sown by hand.	Seed-drill sowed and covered seeds.
Hoeing was done by hand.	The horse hoe lifted weeds and dropped them off.
Most small farmers lived in poverty.	Most small farmers had to sell up and became labourers.
All on the land had some work.	Machinery made many labourers unemployed.
Poor, young farmers had a home.	Young labourers lived in bothies.

page learnt

Changes in working conditions in the textile industry

1. Spinning

• The domestic system

In 1750 all spinning was done by **hand** on simple spinning wheels by skilled women in their homes. They had to work for many hours to produce what their merchants had ordered. They could work when they wanted and do other work, e.g. feeding animals or going to market. If they were ill, they could catch up later. If they lived on the land, they were controlled only by the seasonal demands of farming – and the need to make some money.

• The factory system

By 1800 spinning was done by **machine** on steam-driven Spinning Jennies, Water Frames or Mules by unskilled women in factories. One Mule could spin 1,200 spindles of thread at the same time. Skilled spinners were no longer needed. Women and children in factories were controlled by the machines. As long as the machines worked, they were compelled to work. Being ill could mean dismissal. The wages were regular but low. Conditions were harsh with strict rules and fines were imposed for breaking them.

2. Weaving

• The domestic system

In 1750 weaving was done on **hand-looms** by skilled men working in their homes. This domestic system lasted longer for weavers than for spinners. In fact, conditions improved for hand-loom weavers during the 18th century because there were no weaving machine inventions then. Indeed, although the number of weavers increased, there was always more thread than weavers could use. They could demand high wages and needed to work only four days a week.

This changed when weaving machines were invented in the early 19th century.

2. Weaving (cont.)

• The factory system

By 1830 **power looms** were being widely used in factories. A power loom operated by unskilled labour could work more cheaply and at twice the speed of a hand-loom weaver. The figures below give some idea of the changing working conditions of weavers.

No. of power looms in Scotland	No. of hand-loom weavers	Weekly wage of hand-loom weavers
2,000 in 1820	84,000 in 1840	£1.35 in 1800
23,000 in 1845	25,000 in 1850	£0.25 in 1840

The plight of the hand-loom weavers was made worse by large numbers of weavers coming from Ireland and the Highlands prepared to work for lower wages.

3. Child labour

By 1830 large numbers of children were employed in the cotton mills as scavengers, piecers and, when older, as spinners. Many worked 16 hours a day for 25p per day. Conditions were hot and the work was exhausting. It was the overseer's job to keep children working at all times. Beatings were frequent.

4. The Factory Acts of 1833, 1844 and 1847

1833 Factory Act
- No children under 9 years old to work
- Children aged 9 to 12 to work no more than 48 hours a week
- Children to have 2 hours of school daily
- Children aged 13 to 17 to work no more than 69 hours a week
- No night work for those under 18 years old

1844 Factory Act
- No children under 8 years old to work
- Children aged 8 to 12 to work $6\frac{1}{2}$ hours daily
- Children aged 13 to 17 to work 12 hours daily

1847 Factory Act
- 12 to 18 year olds and women to work 10 hours daily (maximum of 58 hours a week)

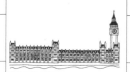

Parliamentary reform up to 1832

1. Electing MPs before 1832

The method of electing MPs before 1832 had not changed for hundreds of years. Parliament did not represent the majority of people in the country. Few people had the vote. Voting was open.

• In Scotland

- Scotland sent 45 MPs to Parliament in 1830: 30 MPs were elected from the counties by about 3,250 real and fictitious voters controlled by landowners; 15 MPs were elected from the burghs by 1,253 self-appointed town councillors.
- There were 4,500 voters in a nation of 2 million people.
- Bribery and corruption at elections were common because there were so few voters and because there was no secret ballot.

• In England and Wales

The method of electing MPs in England and Wales was as bad as and even more complicated than in Scotland.
- Rotten boroughs (places where the population had fallen) still sent 2 MPs to Parliament.
- Pocket boroughs (constituencies where the voters were controlled by landowners) still sent 2 MPs to Parliament.
- The right to vote varied from one borough and county to another.

As a result, only 1 man in 12 in Britain had the vote before 1832.

2. Pressure for reform

There was great demand throughout Britain for the reform of Parliament. Several major incidents demanding reform took place, including demonstrations at **Peterloo** and **Bonnymuir**.

• Peterloo

A crowd of over 60,000 people gathered in St Peter's Fields, Manchester in 1819, to hear speakers including 'Orator' Hunt talk about Parliamentary reform. The meeting was peaceful. Families attended in their best clothes. The magistrates feared a riot and instructed the local militia, the Manchester Yeomanry, to break up the crowd. As a result, 11 people were killed and hundreds injured. Hunt was arrested.

• Peterloo (cont.)

Although the country was shocked, the government continued its policy of **repression**.

• Bonnymuir

The **Radical War** broke out in Scotland in 1820. The Radicals were those who wanted reform of the parliamentary system. There were many causes, but only one solution – the reform of Parliament.

The causes of distress were the bad effects of changes in agriculture and industry, the high cost of food (especially bread), taxation, unemployment and the decline of the hand-loom weavers.

A general strike took place in Glasgow. The **Radical Address** was read throughout central Scotland. A group of workers marching from Glasgow to the Carron Iron Works, near Falkirk, was met by government troops at Bonnymuir. Several marchers were killed. The leaders were arrested. John Baird and Andrew Hardie were hanged and 18 others were transported.

3. The Great Reform Act, 1832

The Great Reform Act, 1832

• Scotland

- In the burghs, votes were given to men owning property worth £10 a year.
- In the counties, votes were given to men owning land worth £10 a year or renting land worth £50 a year.
- Eight more MPs were given to the new industrial towns.
- 65,000 men (1 in 8) could now vote.

• England and Wales

- In the boroughs, votes were given to men owning property worth £10 a year.
- In the counties, votes were given to men owning land worth £2 a year or renting land worth £10 a year.
- 143 seats were taken away from Rotten and Pocket boroughs. These seats went to larger counties and new industrial towns, e.g. Manchester.
- Almost 600,000 men (1 in 7) could now vote.

4. After 1832

- The majority of adult men still could not vote.
- The working class could not vote.
- Middle class merchants and industrialists could vote.
- Voting was still open. Corruption was still common.
- Landowners still controlled MPs.
- Owning property remained vital.

page learnt

3. Changing Life in Scotland and Britain: 1830s – 1930s

Technological change in coal mining

1. Growth in mining

• *Mining in Britain*

During the 19th and early 20th centuries, coal mining in Britain grew dramatically in importance. In 1830 only 30 million tons of coal were mined in Britain, while 270 million tons were mined in 1910.

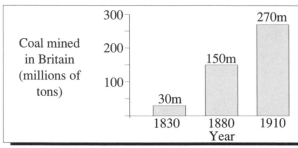

In 1851 there were only 219,000 miners in Britain. This had more than doubled, however, to 504,000 by 1881 and doubled again to 1,094,000 by 1910.

• *Mining in Scotland*

There were 53,741 miners in Scotland in 1881. In 1820, 5% of British coal was mined in Scotland. This had grown to 20% by 1850.

2. Reasons for increased demand for coal

• To drive steam-powered machinery in factories
• For use in the iron industry
• To drive railway engines and steam ships
• Invention of gas lighting
• Vast increase in coal exports
• Domestic population increased

3. Results for mining

• Coal mines had to be dug deeper.
• Coal mining became a more dangerous job.

4. Dangers and improvements

Danger	Improvement	Introduced
Flooding	Newcomen's and Watt's steam pump	After 1780
Poisonous gas	Safety lamp	After 1820
Fire damp – explosive gas	Safety lamp	After 1820
Roof falls	Pit props and better engineering	After 1850
Hauling coal to the surface	Use of wire rope and steam engines	After 1850
Coal hand-cut	Electric cutting machines	After 1910

☐ page learnt

Technological change in the railways

There was a boom in railway building in the 1830s – a 'railway mania'.

1. Effects of the railways

• Travel by rail was cheaper, quicker and more comfortable than by horse-drawn coach.

• Canals declined. Railways did not suffer from freezing or drought and were faster.

• Coastal shipping declined.

• Fresh food could be taken anywhere in Britain.

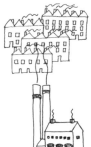

• New and older towns grew if they were near a railway line. Others, which were not, declined.

• Factories, e.g. in Glasgow, were built near railway lines for transporting finished goods.

• The working classes began to take holidays by the sea.

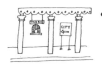

• The middle classes could live in suburbs and travel to work by train.

• Employment of 100,000 people by 1860.

• Improved communications – therefore better postal service and newspaper distribution. This helped trade unionism to grow.

• The whole of Britain went onto a standard time.

2. Construction of the railways

- **1830s**

  The railways were built by navvies, most of whom were from Ireland. They were hardworking, highly paid, wandering labourers. They could move 20 tons a day, work with explosives and lived in danger of rock-falls and cave-ins. They had their own tools and used little machinery.

- **1890s**

  There was extensive use of machinery, especially for cutting and tunnelling. There was still a large labour force. Few natural obstacles could not be tackled by the great engineers, e.g. the Forth Railway Bridge was built in 1890.

Health and housing in the towns

1. Poor conditions in 1830

*(See also "**Health and housing in the towns**", on pages 6 and 7.)*

Life was hard for most of the population of Britain in 1830. The upper class and the growing urban middle classes, however, saw their living standards improve as the country became increasingly wealthy. But for those who worked in the factories, foundries and mines, housing was substandard. Poor health remained a threat to life.

The government believed that it was not right to interfere in the work of private individuals, e.g. factory owners. This policy of non-interference was called ***laissez faire***. There were few laws to protect tenants or workers. They lived in overcrowded rented accommodation, which was often tied to their job.

- If a worker lost his job, he was usually evicted.
- The majority of owners built flats as cheaply as possible.
- Maintaining or upgrading the property was seldom a priority.
- Large families, living in two rooms, with a lodger to help pay the rent, were common.
- Overcrowding remained the main cause of the rapid spread of diseases, especially cholera, in towns.

2. Burgh Reform Act, 1833

> ### Burgh Reform Act, 1833
> *Money from the rates paid to Scottish town councils was to be used for cleaning the streets, preventing disease and making sure slaughterhouses followed strict rules. This Act was added to and its provisions were made compulsory during the rest of the 19th century.*

3. Public Health Act, 1848

> ### Public Health Act, 1848
> *This Act was the result of the Royal Commission Report of 1842 into the Sanitary Conditions of the Labouring Classes and the cholera outbreak in 1848. The Act was a failure.*
> - *A Central Board of Health was established to set up local Health Boards.*
> - *The Central Board could make recommendations to local Boards, but could not force them to act.*
> - *Few local Boards were set up, so most of the population remained unprotected.*
>
> *The Central Board was abolished in 1858.*

Edwin Chadwick, the first Secretary of the Royal Commission and a member of the Board of Health, continued to campaign for better sewage systems, the removal of refuse, improved housing and a proper water supply. After 1848 some large cities were given government permission to clear the worst of their slums. London improved its water supply and covered open sewers.

4. Public Health Act, 1875

> ### Public Health Act, 1875
> *Local authorities had to appoint a Medical Officer in charge of public health.*
> - *A local sanitary inspector was appointed to supervise slaughterhouses and destroy contaminated food.*
> - *Local authorities were ordered to:*
>   - *cover sewers and keep them in good condition*
>   - *provide a clean water supply*
>   - *pave, clean and light the streets*
>   - *collect refuse.*

page learnt

5. Little change

A Royal Commission Report on Housing in 1918 found that many of the poor conditions which had existed a century before were still common in towns and cities throughout the country.

More than 50% of Scots lived in one- or two-roomed houses in 1911 (compared to 7% of the population of England).

Health and housing in the countryside

(*See also "Health and housing in the countryside" on page 7.*)

1. Housing improvements after 1850

In **1830** housing in the countryside for the majority of Scots was very poor. Single men lived in bothies. Families who laboured lived in one- or two-roomed houses with stone walls, earth floors and roofs of turf.

After **1850** many landlords rebuilt and improved the cottages on their land. However, landlords charged higher rents for the cottages. Not all workers could afford them because their wages were still too low.

2. Poor health

Most of the population was unhealthy because they

- had a poor and monotonous diet – broth, bread, oatmeal and potatoes were the staple foods.

- lived in damp and badly ventilated houses.

- worked long hours in all weathers.

- could not afford doctors' fees. (Doctors charged money to treat patients then.)

3. Other improvements

Improvements were made in public health by slum clearance, by building new hospitals in major towns and by medical discoveries, e.g. chloroform and antiseptics. However, progress in health and housing was slow between 1830 and 1930.

Changes in working conditions on the land

1. Change

In **1830** one million people worked on farms in England and Wales. In Scotland, two thirds of the population were involved in agriculture. The average farm worker's wage was £4 per year. Labourers worked outside six days a week from dawn to dusk, with inside work being done after that.

By **1860** things were changing. Nearly every farm in Lothian used steam engines for ploughing and threshing. There were fewer jobs and wages for labourers fell.

2. Golden Age

Britain was entering its Golden Age of Farming by 1860. For a few years, although food prices were high, those who still had jobs on farms could pay their rent.

This Golden Age did not last long, however. A period of depression began after 1870. There were 25% fewer jobs in farming by 1914.

Farmers who grew wheat found they were hit by foreign competition. For once, ordinary farm workers benefited as shown by the cost of a 4 lb loaf:

Cost of a 4 lb loaf

1880 – 3p
1890 – 2½p
1900 – 1p

3. Change from wheat growing

Those farmers who changed to producing meat, milk, butter, cheese and vegetables prospered. Those who changed to growing fruit also did well. The amount of land used for growing fruit doubled between 1873 and 1907.

4. Prosperity then decline

During World War I farmers prospered. They were paid large subsidies to feed the country. However, by 1920 agriculture again declined. This decline continued until the start of World War II.

5. New technology

Richer farmers quickly embraced the new technology. Tractors became common in the 1920s and oil and petrol engines replaced horse and manpower.

Changes in working conditions in coal mines

1. Hard and dangerous work

Throughout the 19th century, coal mining was a hard and dangerous job. Many miners could earn more than factory workers, but accidents were common which resulted in no income at all. Mine owners were reluctant to install expensive machinery because labour was cheap and plentiful.

After the Factory Act of 1833 the government set up a number of inquiries into mining which led to a Royal Commission, whose illustrated report shocked Parliament.

2. Royal Commission Report, 1842

- Children were working up to 14 hours a day.
- Women and children were used as bearers to carry 1 cwt (50 kg) bags.
- Children were used as trappers sitting in complete darkness all day.
- Children had to work in narrow coal seams which were often damp.
- Beatings were common.

3. The Mines Act, 1842

The Mines Act, 1842
- *No women or girls to work underground.*
- *No boys under 10 years old to work underground.*
- *No child under 15 years old to be left in charge of machinery.*
- *Inspectors were appointed. (More were appointed in 1850.)*

4. Continued danger

- In 1870 boys were still doing the type of work that had been condemned 30 years before. Many of the old dangers of suffocation, snapping of winding gear and explosions were still present.
- 600,000 workers between 1922 and 1924 were involved in accidents in mining – an industry which still employed under-age children.

5. Improvements

- Mine owners started to introduce new machinery between 1900 and 1930. Most coal in Scotland was cut by hand before 1914; by 1928 60% was cut mechanically.
- Some began to provide baths for their workers after the **Coal Mines Act** of **1911** was passed.

6. Strikes

Miners went on strike for seven months in 1926 after owners tried to reduce their wages in order to cut their own costs. The subsidies the mine owners had received during World War I had ended and the demand for their coal had declined. This was because of foreign competition and the exhaustion of easily mined surface coal seams.

Parliamentary reform after 1832

1. The first step

The Great Reform Act had been passed in 1832. Many politicians did not wish any more reform of Parliament.

Processions demanding reform of Parliament

However, other people who had not received the vote wanted more reform. For them, 1832 was only the first step.

2. William Gladstone

Gladstone's attention was drawn to the urban skilled working class in the growing towns and cities of Britain. He came to realise that a loyal, honest, thrifty working class man existed who deserved to have a share in political power. Lord Palmerston, the Prime Minister, was against giving working men the vote. When he died in 1865, Gladstone convinced other Liberals in his party that it was time for a change.

3. Gladstone's 1866 Bill

Gladstone said that the vote should be given to those who lived in houses rated at £7 a year. This was opposed by many politicians, including some from Gladstone's own party.

4. The Second Reform Act, 1867

After Gladstone's Reform Bill was defeated, Lord Derby was asked to form a Conservative government. Benjamin Disraeli led the government in the House of Commons. He realised that Parliamentary reform was inevitable.

page learnt

4. The Second Reform Act, 1867 (cont.)

The Second Reform Act, 1867

- *Terms – Voting*
  - *In towns, male house owners over 21.*
  - *In towns, male lodgers who paid £10 a year in rent.*
  - *In counties, males who owned property worth £5 a year.*
  - *In counties, males who rented property worth £12 a year (£14 in Scotland).*
- *Terms – Seats*
  - *35 boroughs lost one of their MPs.*
  - *17 boroughs lost both MPs.*
  - *Counties were given 25 extra MPs.*
  - *Large cities were given a third MP.*
- *Results*
  - *1.12 million new voters.*
  - *Britain moved closer to democracy.*
  - *Bribery and corruption continued.*

5. Other Acts

Secret Ballot Act, 1872
- *Voters could now vote in secret.*

Corrupt and Illegal Practices Act, 1883
- *Election expenses were limited by the size of the constituency.*
- *Illegal and corrupt practices were defined.*
- *Corruption practised during an election could result in imprisonment.*

Third Reform Act, 1884 (Representation of the People Act)
- *Terms*

  This Act gave the vote to male house owners, lodgers and tenants who had lived in a house valued at £10 for at least a year.
- *Results*
  - *The electorate increased from 2.5 to 5 million.*
  - *In Scotland and England 2 out of 3 men could now vote.*

Redistribution of Seats Act, 1885
- *Aim*
  - *to make constituencies equal in size*
- *Results*
  - *79 towns lost both MPs.*
  - *36 towns lost one MP.*
  - *Increase in seats from 652 to 670.*

Representation of the People Act, 1918 and Parliamentary Reform Act, 1928
For these Acts and women's suffrage, see page 20.

For these Acts and women's suffrage, see page 20.

6. Voting Increase

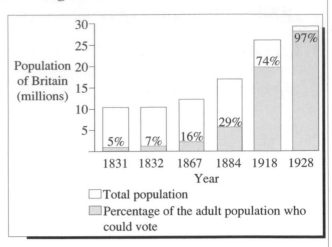

Only 5% of the British population could vote in 1831. This had increased to 97% by 1928.

7. Summary of the steps to reform

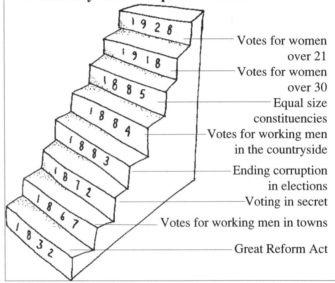

- 1928 — Votes for women over 21
- 1918 — Votes for women over 30
- 1885 — Equal size constituencies
- 1884 — Votes for working men in the countryside
- 1883 — Ending corruption in elections
- 1872 — Voting in secret
- 1867 — Votes for working men in towns
- 1832 — Great Reform Act

4. Changing Life in Scotland and Britain: 1880s – Present Day

Technological change in shipbuilding

1. Scotland's tradition
Scotland had built up a long tradition of shipbuilding by the early 20th century. 20% of the world's ships were built in Scotland in 1914.

2. Change
The methods of building ships changed during the 19th and 20th centuries. Some of these changes are outlined below.

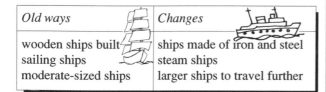

Old ways	Changes
wooden ships built	ships made of iron and steel
sailing ships	steam ships
moderate-sized ships	larger ships to travel further

3. Reasons for growth in Scottish shipbuilding after 1880
- There was a source of cheap steel.
- Deep, sheltered rivers for launching ships
- Scottish expertise in building steam-turbine engines
- A skilled Scottish workforce
- Expansion of the Royal Navy, 1906 – 14
- Ships sunk in World War I needed to be replaced.

4. Decline
By the 1920s, however, the industry was in decline. Thousands of workers were laid off. When the Depression began in 1929, things became even worse. Many shipyards closed.

5. Reasons for decline in the 1920s
- No government subsidies, unlike Germany and Japan
- Collapse of Scottish fishing industry
- Absence of Royal Navy orders in peacetime
- Markets lost in wartime not recovered
- Clyde's failure to build its own turbines
- Decline in demand for large passenger liners

6. Reasons for recovery from the late 1930s
- The need for Royal Navy ships for World War II
- Replacement of ships sunk during the war
- The need for larger tankers between 1945 and 1955.

7. Decline again in Britain
- *Decline*

  After 1955 the industry went into decline once again. The worldwide slump ended in the early 1960s. Shipbuilding in other countries recovered and prospered again. In Britain, however, it did not. In 1945 Britain built 50% of the world's ships; by 1985 that figure had dropped to 2%.

- *Government policy*

  The Labour government **nationalised** the British shipbuilding industry in 1977. The Conservative government had a different attitude to supporting the shipbuilding industry in 1982, but it had little effect:

Year	Government	No. of shipbuilding workers	Losses
1977	Labour	86,000	£106 million
1982	Conservative	66,000	£100 million

8. Reasons for decline in Britain since 1955
- Difficulties in obtaining steel
- The slow rate of work and delays in completion
- A reluctance to adopt new technology
- Rules on demarcation and restrictive practices
- Difficulties in recruiting trained staff
- Rising costs
- Poor management and failure to attract customers
- Foreign competition

page learnt

Technological change in road transport

1. The development of the motor car

took off in the 1880s. Only the rich could afford a car then. In the 1890s electric trams replaced horse-drawn ones in the cities. The streets of Britain were changing as new technology improved methods of travel.

Mass production techniques reached Britain from the USA during World War I and spread after 1920. The resulting reduction in price allowed the middle classes to buy cars. Between 1921 and 1938 rail passenger numbers fell by 40%. For the rest of the 20th century the car has both brought benefits and posed problems for society, e.g. faster transportation, but increased traffic on the roads.

2. Solutions to traffic problems

- New houses were to include a driveway and a garage.
- Streets in new estates were to be wide enough for parked cars and two-way traffic.
- Towns and cities were to create new methods for directing traffic.
- A Ministry of Transport was set up in 1919.

- Petrol stations began to appear.
- Traffic lights were introduced in 1926 and Belisha Beacons in 1934.
- Speed limits were imposed: 1896 – 12 mph; 1903 – 20 mph.

- The 30 mph speed limit was re-introduced in built-up areas, but only after road deaths had reached 7,000 a year.

3. Advantages of motorised transport

- Motor vehicles could go anywhere.
- Motor transport was faster over short distances.
- Remote country areas became more accessible to goods and services.
- Delivery vans meant shops could travel to customers.
- Bus services appeared all over the country.

4. During World War II

Car production stopped. The car industry was used to make aeroplanes. The methods of mass production could build planes faster than aircraft manufacturers could ever have achieved.

5. During the 1960s and 1970s

- *Bad reputation*

The British car industry had a bad reputation for
- workers being laid off for long periods
- strikes
- high prices
- poor quality
- late delivery.

- *Results*
- People bought foreign cars.
- Order books were full, but companies still made losses because of out of date technology and overmanning.
- Stiff new management methods were introduced – 70,000 redundancies, but huge losses continued.
- Government subsidies ended in the 1980s.

6. The effects of technology, 1945 – Present Day

- 1950s and 60s – people wanted speed and style
1970s and 80s – people wanted safety and economy

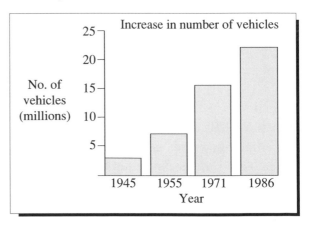

- Increase in number of vehicles
- 91% of journeys were made by road transport in 1986
- Increase in pedestrian precincts – separating the car from the pedestrian
- Increase in one-way traffic in towns and cities
- Increase in motorway construction
- The dismantling of the railways in the 1960s brought large lorries into towns and villages.

Housing in the towns

1. Divided

In 1880 Britain was a socially divided nation. Health and housing standards among the upper and middle classes were very good. They lived in large houses able to accommodate servants. For the majority of people, however, things were different. A **Royal Commission on Housing** in **1884 - 5** concluded that the drains, water supply, buildings and sanitation were as bad in many places in 1880 as they had been in 1830. *(See also page 11.)*

2. Housing Acts

were passed after 1890 to clear slums. 250,000 were cleared by 1939, but 500,000 still remained. After 1918 council housing estates began to be built across the country.

3. New houses

The government could never meet its targets for house building. In 1945 Britain needed 1.25 million new houses. Only 1 million had been built by 1950 when even more were needed than in 1945. £150 million was spent on **Prefabs**.

4. 1960s – Present Day

- A boom in private house building. A decline in council house building.
- Governments believed that all health and housing problems could be cured by building New Towns.
- Over 20% of council houses have been sold in Britain and over 200,000 have been sold in Scotland.

Housing in the countryside

A **Royal Commission Report** of **1893** stated that health and housing had generally improved in the countryside. Still, many problems remained. Houses commonly had:
- no running water or sanitation;
- fewer than three rooms;
- floors made of earth.

Health in the towns and countryside

The major killer diseases, e.g. cholera, typhoid and typhus, had been tackled by 1880. However, the general health of the country remained poor. In 1903 one in every three recruits for the army was rejected on health grounds. Death in early childhood was still a serious problem.

1. The Liberal Reforms, 1906 – 14

The Liberal Reforms, 1906 – 14
- *Free school meals for needy children.*
- *Free medical inspection and treatment for children.*
- *The National Health Insurance Act, 1911 provided unemployment and sickness insurance for the low paid.*

In 1936 a survey stated that 30% of the population did not have a balanced diet and 10% were severely undernourished.

2. The Welfare State

The Beveridge Report and the National Health Act, 1946
- *A free National Health Service.*
- *The nationalisation of all hospitals.*
- *Regional Health Boards set up.*
- *Local authorities responsible for maternity and child welfare, home nursing and schools' medicals.*
- *Private medical care could remain for those who could afford it.*

3. Results

- The work of the Labour government brought an end to many years of *laissez faire (see page 11).*
- 187 million prescriptions and 8.5 million dental treatments had been given by 1947.
- Killer diseases, e.g. TB, have been wiped out. (Others, however, e.g. cancer and AIDS, have replaced them.)
- The cost of the NHS soared from £388 million in 1949 to £2,270 million in 1971 and £16,300 million in 1985.
- 95% of the population use the National Health Service today.
- Long waiting lists for NHS hospital treatment have contributed to four million people taking out private medical insurance in the last decade.

page learnt

Changes in working conditions for women

1. Inequality

In 1880 the most common occupations for women were:

• *domestic service*
working 14 hours a day with very little time off.

• *sweated labour*
- seamstresses working 16 hours a day for 1p per hour.
- brick making and chain making – heavy, manual labour.
- match girls, 20p per week.

Match Girls at work

When women did the same jobs as men, they earned less than half the pay.

By the start of the 20th century women were able to enter medicine and teaching. If a woman teacher married, however, she had to give up her job.

2. Reasons for some change

• *Trade unions*
Women were encouraged to join trade unions to achieve better conditions.

• *Education*
- The Education Acts of 1902 and 1918 gave more opportunity to girls.
- The expansion of education meant more teachers were needed. 65% of Scottish teachers in 1914 were women.

• *The Suffrage movement*
Part of this struggle was for equality in the workplace.

• *World War I*
Women did men's jobs successfully.

• *World War II*
Women's contribution to the war effort was even greater than in 1914 – 18.

2. Reasons for some change (cont.)

• *Changes in industry after 1945*
The growth of service and light industries gave jobs to thousands of women.

• *Acts of Parliament*
- Equal Pay Act, 1970
- Sex Discrimination Act, 1975

• *The work of the Equal Opportunities Commission*

3. Lack of other change

• In 1881, 136,000 women were domestic servants; in 1931, 138,000 were domestic servants.

• In 1900 women still dominated the unskilled, low-paid textile industry.

• In 1914 male teachers earned twice as much as female.

• In 1975 male manual and non-manual workers earned almost twice as much as female.

• Today men still dominate the professions and the key jobs in Britain.

The role of trade unions

After the **Third Reform Act** of **1884**, trade unions campaigned to have working men elected to Parliament. They also fought for higher wages and for better conditions for working people.

1. Strikes

• *1888*   Match Girls' Strike

• *1889*   London Dockers' Strike

• *1889 – 90* 'New' unions set up for unskilled workers, e.g. textile and builders' labourers.

• *1911 – 14* Many strikes, doubling of membership. 'Triple Alliance' of miners, railway and transport workers.

2. Trade union membership

grew dramatically between 1888 and 1978.

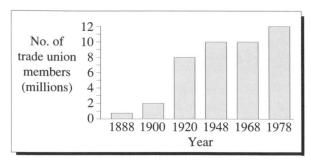

In 1888 there were 750,000 trade union members; by 1978 this had increased to 12 million.

3. The General Strike, 1926

- *1921*

  Miners' wages cut by mine owners. Unsuccessful three-month strike by miners.

- *1925*

  Further wage cuts threatened. Government appointed the Samuel Commission to examine coal industry. The Commission recommended reorganisation and improvements in conditions. It also said wage cuts were necessary.

- *1926*

  General Strike, 3 – 12 May. Supported by the TUC. Three million workers on strike. Although the General Strike ended on 12 May, miners stayed on strike for a further seven months, but without the support of the TUC.

- *1927*

  Trade Dispute Act. General strikes made illegal; civil servants banned from joining the TUC.

4. Trade unions and the Labour Party

After the failure of the 1926 General Strike, the trade union movement worked with the Labour Party to bring about social reform. They realised change could only come about through Parliament. The Labour Party worked closely with the TU movement during its early governments.

In the 1960s and 70s, however, the relationship became a problem. The power of the TU movement was at its height. The increase in strikes in the 1970s is seen as one important reason for having kept the Labour Party in opposition since 1979.

Parliamentary reform and women's suffrage after 1884

1. Parliamentary reform since 1884

After the Third Reform Act *(see page 14)*, all women and 40% of men could still not vote. Women had been trying to get the vote since 1867. In 1867 the town-dwelling male working class were given the vote. Women immediately demanded the same rights.

A few improvements in women's rights did take place, but progress was slow:

- *1880*
  - Women could vote in local elections.
  - Women could keep their own property.

- *1894*

  Women could become local councillors.

2. The Suffragette Campaign

In 1903 Emmeline Pankhurst founded the **Women's Social and Political Union**.

- *Peaceful tactics*

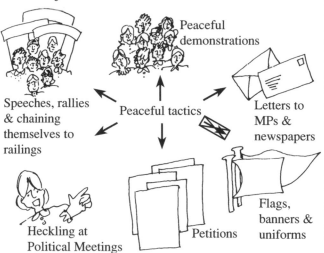

- *1905*

  Suffragettes active in the General Election campaign.

- *1905 – 14*

  Suffragettes campaign against Liberal Government which was divided on the issue of women's suffrage.

- *1907*

  200,000 in Suffragette march in London.

- *1909*

  First hunger strike and force-feeding. Force-feeding caused national outcry.

page learnt

2. The Suffragette Campaign (cont.)
• *Militant tactics*

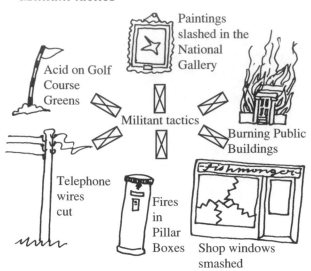

- *1912*

  Violent campaign began, led by Christabel Pankhurst.

- *1913*

  Emily Wilding Davison fatally injured at the 'Suffragette Derby' by jumping in front of the King's horse on Derby Day.

- *1913*

  Government passed the **Prisoners' Temporary Discharge for Ill-Health Act**, known as the 'Cat and Mouse Act'. This allowed the release from prison of women who had made themselves ill in prison by hunger strikes. When they recovered, they were rearrested to complete their jail sentences.

- *1914*

  Outbreak of World War I – Suffragette campaign stopped.

3. Parliament's reaction

- The majority of MPs were against giving women the vote.

- The government believed that there were more important issues to deal with.

- When militancy began, the government became determined to resist force.

- Many thought that militancy showed women to be irresponsible.

- Many Liberals thought that women would vote for the Conservatives.

4. World War I

temporarily removed the problem. The Suffragette campaign stopped. Large numbers of women were employed in essential war work.

Women's contribution to the war effort had a greater effect in gaining them the vote than the Suffragette campaign.

5. Votes for women

> ***Representation of the People Act, 1918***
>
> *Women over 30 years old who were householders or wives of householders got the vote.*
>
> ***Parliamentary Reform Act, 1928***
> *Women over 21 years old got the vote.*
> *Women now had the same voting rights as men.*

The causes of World War I

The four chief causes of World War I were: **M**ilitarism, the system of **A**lliances, **I**mperialism and **N**ationalism (MAIN*).
(* *The word 'MAIN' is made up of the first letters of the four chief causes of World War I. It is called a mnemonic. Making up mnemonics is a good way to remember information. Make up other mnemonics when you are working through these Notes.*)

1. The System of Alliances

Before 1914 Europe was divided into two armed camps. The six major powers made treaties with each other. The map shows the two hostile groups.

▨ Triple Entente
▨ Triple Alliance

- **The Triple Alliance** – Germany, Austria-Hungary and Italy.
  - *1879* Germany and Austria-Hungary agreed to support each other if Russia attacked.
  - *1882* Italy joined in when it fell out with France over who controlled Tunis in North Africa.
- **The Triple Entente** – Great Britain, France and Russia.
  - *1894* France and Russia formed the Dual Alliance.
  - *1904* France and Britain signed the *Entente Cordiale* (friendly understanding).
  - *1907* Together, the three countries formed the Triple Entente.

2. Militarism

- **The Naval Race**
  As the alliances developed, so did the armed forces of the major powers. Germany had the most powerful army in Europe.

- **The Naval Race (cont.)**
  It decided to build up its navy. This was seen by Britain as a challenge. The greatest competition in the naval race between Britain and Germany was over the Dreadnought battleship. By 1914 Britain had 29 Dreadnoughts, while Germany had 17.

- **Britain's need for a powerful navy**
  - Britain was an island. If an invasion took place, it would be by sea. A strong navy was needed to protect Britain's shores.
  - In a war Britain might be attacked by more than one country. It wanted its navy to be bigger than its nearest two rivals put together.
  - As an island, Britain depended on its merchant fleet to bring food from overseas. This fleet had to be protected.
  - Britain had a vast empire. A large navy was needed to defend it.

3. Nationalism in the Balkans

As the Ottoman Empire fell to pieces, Russia and Austria-Hungary tried to extend their influence in the Balkans. In 1908 Austria-Hungary annexed Bosnia-Herzegovina.

At the same time, many Slav nationalist groups within Austria-Hungary wanted independence. They looked to independent Serbia for help. Austria-Hungary wanted Serbia crushed. Serbia became stronger after defeating the Turks in the First Balkan War, 1912 and other Balkan states in the Second Balkan War, 1913.

By 1914 resentment between Austria-Hungary and Serbia was at its height.

4. Imperialism

- **Imperial rivalry**
  Britain and France had the two largest empires in the world. Germany wanted 'a place in the sun' to build up its wealth and international prestige. Germany's desire for more colonies was seen by Britain and France as a threat.

- **Economic rivalry**
  Britain was losing its position as the world's leading industrial country by 1900. Trading markets were being lost to Germany.

page learnt ☐

5. International crises

• *Assassination*
A number of international crises took place between 1905 and 1914 which made relations between countries more hostile. The worst was the assassination of the Austro-Hungarian Archduke Franz Ferdinand on 28 June 1914 in Sarajevo, the capital of Bosnia. The assassin was a Serbian student, Gavrilo Princip. Austria-Hungary took this as an opportunity to crush Serbia. Austria-Hungary delivered an **ultimatum** to Serbia, which, if accepted, would have meant the end of an independent Serbia. Serbia rejected the ultimatum.

• *War declared*
Austria-Hungary then declared war on Serbia. Russia declared war on Austria-Hungary in support of Serbia. Germany, in support of its ally Austria-Hungary, declared war on Russia and France.

• *Invasion*
It was only when Germany invaded Belgium that Britain declared war on Germany and Austria-Hungary on 4 August, 1914.

The experience of war on the Western Front

1. The beginning of the War in 1914

• *Britain declares war*
Britain declared war on Germany on 4 August 1914. The Treaty of London of 1839 which guaranteed Belgian independence had been broken by Germany when it invaded Belgium. Britain was bound to protect Belgian neutrality.

• *Kitchener's volunteers*
The British Expeditionary Force (BEF) consisting of 100,000 men left for France. Lord Kitchener, the Minister of War, called for another 100,000 volunteers. Over 500,000 volunteered in the first few weeks.

• *Over by Christmas?*
Generals on both sides expected a war of movement with cavalry and infantry attacks in the west. The millions of Russian soldiers would 'steamroll' the German armies in the east. The Germans expected the Schlieffen Plan to knock out the French in six weeks, leaving them to move east and fight on until the Russians were defeated. Everyone expected that the war would be over by Christmas. This did not happen.

1. The beginning of the War in 1914 (cont.)

• *Deadlock*
Both sides had incurred half a million casualties and had reached a deadlock by the end of 1914. They began to dig in to secure their positions. The war of movement had ended. Trench warfare had begun.

2. Trench warfare

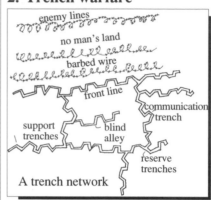

A trench network

• *Trench networks*
A complex network of trenches was dug on the Western Front. They stretched from the English Channel to the Swiss border. This was now a war of defence, not a war of attack. It became a war of attrition.

• *Conditions in the trenches*
were appalling. They were

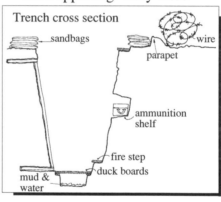

Trench cross section

- flooded trenches
- living in all weathers – trench feet
- rats and lice in their millions
- the continual noise of shelling
- the fear of artillery bombardment
- the dread of being shot by snipers
- advances made under enemy machine gun fire and through barbed wire
- the effects of gas attacks
- bare rations of bully beef and hard biscuits
- enormous casualties
- coping with the death of friends.

• *Daily routine*
- weapon cleaning and inspection
- digging and repairing trenches
- mending the barbed wire
- spying on enemy activity
- removing the dead and wounded
- bringing up rations and supplies
- tunnelling and mining to set charges
- delousing.

page learnt

The experience of war on the British Home Front

Although no fighting took place on British or German soil, those who remained at home had a large part to play in helping to fight the war.

1. Patriotism

There was a great burst of patriotism in Britain in August 1914. There was also widespread anti-German feeling.

Over 500,000 responded to Kitchener's call for volunteers. Those who volunteered believed the war would be over by Christmas.

2. Opposition to the War

There was a small but important current of feeling against the war.
Conscientious objectors and pacifists had to appear before a military tribunal to declare and defend their beliefs. If they were turned down by the tribunal, they were arrested as deserters, courtmartialled and imprisoned. Many agreed to join the non-combatant corps and became stretcher bearers, ambulance drivers and trench diggers. Those who refused spent the war in prison.

3. Women at war

Women made a vital contribution to winning World War I by working in a wide variety of jobs.

- ### WRNS (Wrens)
The **Women's Royal Naval Service** was formed in November 1917. It took over shore duties from the Royal Navy. The Wrens cleaned torpedoes, decoded messages, and made mine-nets, depth charges and sails, in addition to cooking and clerical work. Some Wrens also served overseas, e.g. in Malta, Gibraltar, Genoa and Ostend.

- ### WAAC
The **Women's Army Auxiliary Corps** was formed in 1917 to release men for the fighting line. The WAACs served as typists, clerks, telephonists and drivers. During the war nearly 60,000 women joined, 10,000 of whom served in France.

3. Women at war (cont.)

- ### WRAF
The **Women's Royal Air Force** was formed in April 1918, at the same time as the Royal Air Force. As with the other women's services, most WRAFs did clerical and domestic work mainly, but some were employed as fitters, riggers, welders and electricians.

- ### VAD Nurses
Voluntary Aid Detachments, whose members were popularly known as VADs, were formed by the Red Cross for various duties, including nursing. At first entirely voluntary, VADs were given some payment as hospital war work increased. Their services were invaluable in dealing with the large numbers of war-wounded.

- ### Munitions workers

More women were employed in munitions work than in any other single industry. By the end of the war over 900,000 'munitionettes' helped to produce guns, aircraft, shells and other types of ammunition. The work could be unpleasant and dangerous – more than 300 women died from TNT poisoning and as a result of explosions.

- ### Land Girls
Although a considerable number of women had been employed in agriculture before 1914, many more were needed to replace the thousands of male farm labourers who joined up. The **Women's Land Army**, formed in 1917, provided women for almost every type of farm work, including ploughing, labouring and livestock farming. There were 230,000 women working on the land in 1918.

- ### Gas Company workers
Women stoked the furnaces, drove steamrollers, made bricks, carried out acetylene welding, built aero-engines and worked overhead cranes. Some jobs demanded considerable physical strength; others depended on technical skills which, in many cases, women were being allowed to develop for the first time.

- ### Transport workers
Well over 117,000 women worked in transport in 1918, compared to only 18,000 in 1914. Female porters, ticket collectors, carriage cleaners, conductors and guards had become a familiar sight on the buses, trams and railways by the end of the war.

page learnt

4. The Defence of the Realm Act, 1914

The Defence of the Realm Act, 1914

Parliament passed D.O.R.A. on 8 August 1914. This Act gave the government the power to control peoples' lives during the war.

- **Censorship**
  Newspapers were censored so that enemy spies could not get information, but also so that the British people could not find out about the horrific military defeats.

- **Aliens**
  Many people lived in Britain who were not born here. If they had been born in an enemy country and had not become British subjects, they were classed as enemy aliens. Failure to register could result in a fine or imprisonment.

- **The sale of alcohol**
  Laws were passed restricting the sale of alcohol and the opening hours of public houses. The price of alcohol was also controlled by the government.

- **Curfews**
  were imposed giving police the right to stop and search anyone out at night without proper authority. People were forbidden to enter certain areas or even buy binoculars without official permission.

- **Industry**
  The Munitions of War Act of 1916 gave complete control of war production to Lloyd George. He could settle disputes, forbid strikes, limit profits and send workers where they were needed.

- **Conscription**
  The Military Service Acts of 1916 made all men between 18 and 41 eligible to be called up for war. There were, however, exemptions for some, e.g. for those still in education or training or involved in vital war work.

5. Air raids and naval bombardments

Attacks on British soil with few casualties often caused more anger at home than did the slaughter on the Western Front.

- A German cruiser force shelled Hartlepool and Scarborough on 16 December 1912. 137 people were killed.

- 57 *Zeppelin* raids on Britain killed 564 civilians and injured 1,370 people.

- A new series of air raids on Britain, using *Gotha* and giant bomber aircraft in 1917 and 1918 caused greater loss of life and damage than the *Zeppelins*.

6. Food supplies and rationing

Some kinds of food were in short supply in Britain from the beginning of the war. After February 1917 Germany's unrestricted submarine warfare campaign caused serious shortages. 2.3 million tons of Allied and neutral shipping were destroyed between January and April 1917.

 The government introduced a number of methods to deal with the shortages:

- Propaganda campaigns encouraged people to avoid waste, eat less and grow more food.

- The allotment system increased the amount of land available for growing food.

- Voluntary rationing introduced in February 1917 encouraged people to limit their food intake.

- Price controls were introduced towards the end of 1917 to keep basic foods available to all.

- The rationing of sugar was introduced in December 1917. Meat and butter were rationed in April 1918. Tea was rationed later in the year.

- Hoarders were prosecuted.

- The convoy system was introduced. Merchant ships were escorted in groups by Royal Navy ships for protection.

The experience of war on the German Home Front

- A naval blockade of German ports was begun immediately war started to prevent supplies reaching the German people.

- Food shortages in Germany were made worse by bad harvests in 1916. Provisions in Germany were in shorter supply than in Britain in 1917.

- Rationing was introduced in Germany in 1915, but this was not as successful as it was in Britain. *Ersatz* (substitute foods) were prepared. While British restaurants had 'meatless days', Germans had to endure 'meatless weeks'. Malnutrition became a serious problem. The results were disease and death.

- Shortages of fuel and raw materials for the war industries were also great.

New technology and its effects on the War

1. A new kind of war

In August 1914 most generals on both sides expected the war to be the same as previous ones – a war of movement with cavalry and infantry attacks. However, industrialists had developed new weapons which were to make World War I different from any previous conflict. Existing weapons had changed out of all recognition.

2. Artillery

Big guns were able to fire over long distances with great accuracy.

The British fired 170 million shells during the four years of war. Before each major battle, massive artillery bombardments would be fired on enemy lines in order to destroy their trenches and the barbed wire. This was seldom achieved. Instead, the barbed wire became even more entangled and **No Man's Land** was made even more difficult to cross.

The only protection against artillery was to dig deeper into the ground. The Germans protected themselves in this way during the week-long preliminary bombardment which started the Battle of the Somme in 1916.

3. Machine guns

The use of the machine gun was devastating. Unlike the Germans, the British disliked it as a weapon in 1914. However, they soon changed their minds. The machine gun contributed more to the stalemate on the Western Front than any other weapon because it pinned down troops on both sides in their trenches.

4. Gas

First used by the Germans on the Eastern Front. Gas was also used in April 1915 during the Second Battle of Ypres. Three types of gas were used:

- *chlorine gas* thousands died of suffocation.

- *phosgene gas* caused suffocation and blindness.

- *mustard gas* slowly destroyed the insides of those who breathed it in until they died.

This led to the invention of gas masks. The wearing of gas masks gradually reduced the use of gas as a weapon in the war.

5. Tanks

Invented by the British, the tank was the most important piece of new warfare technology. They were first used during the Battle of the Somme in September 1916, but not in sufficient numbers to bring about a victory. They had a greater effect at the Battle of Cambrai which was fought on chalk soil, instead of the mud at the Somme. However, tanks can only take land – they cannot hold it. At Cambrai there were too few infantrymen to hold the land and so the chance of a quick victory was lost.

Too often tanks became stuck, overheated or just broke down.

6. Armour-piercing shells

When tanks were first used, they were believed to be invincible. However, German armour-piercing shells proved that to be wrong.

7. Shrapnel shells

Shells containing shrapnel were designed to explode before hitting the ground. The explosion sent out hundreds of metal balls or small pieces of iron in all directions to kill, maim or injure.

8. Barbed wire

was invented by the Americans in the 19th century. Factories in the countries at war produced thousands of miles of barbed wire to protect their trenches. Many soldiers on both sides died entangled in it.

9. Periscopes

A constant fear of every soldier in the trenches was the enemy sniper. The periscope allowed observation into No Man's Land without putting one's head above the parapet. However, trained snipers learned to look for the glinting of the glass.

10. Aeroplanes

were only used at first for aerial spotting of enemy trenches – troop movements, the build up of supplies and the movement of weapons. Later in the war, they were used as combat aircraft and in bombing raids.

11. Observation balloons

were also used for aerial spotting because most of the Western Front was flat land. Their major advantage was that they were cheaper to replace than aeroplanes.

page learnt

The Treaty of Versailles and the treatment of Germany

1. Allied Demands

Germany and the Allies signed an armistice (ceasefire) which began at 11a.m. on 11 November 1918. Although World War I was over, a final Peace Treaty still had to be signed. The Allies prepared for this and insisted on a number of preconditions.

Allied Demands

- *The Kaiser had to abdicate. The Allied leaders refused to deal with him.*
- *Germany had to become a republic with a civilian government.*
- *The German army had to withdraw from all occupied territory.*
- *All prisoners of war had to be returned.*
- *The German High Seas Fleet had to surrender.*
- *The west bank of the Rhine had to be evacuated.*

Although the German delegates were shocked, the conditions had to be accepted. The Allies threatened to march on Berlin if they were not.

2. The peacemakers

In January 1919 fifty-one Allied leaders gathered in the Palace of Versailles, outside Paris. The four main leaders were:

- President Woodrow Wilson of the United States
- Prime Minister David Lloyd George of Great Britain
- Prime Minister Georges Clemenceau of France
- Prime Minister Vittorio Orlando of Italy.

These four dominated the peace discussions. It was sometimes difficult to remember that they were on the same side. Their aims were very different.

3. The differing aims of the peacemakers

• President Wilson

was an idealist. He wanted a just and honourable peace concluded with Germany. He wanted to solve the problems which had caused the war so that war would never happen again. He did not want the USA to be involved in any more European wars.

3. The differing aims of the peacemakers (cont.)

• Prime Minister Lloyd George

wanted Germany punished, but not crippled. He believed that Germany would want revenge if it was crippled. He wanted Germany to be able to become once again a healthy trading partner for buying British goods.

• Prime Minister Clemenceau

France had suffered most of all. Germany had invaded France twice in the last fifty years. France wanted security against any future aggression by its neighbour. Clemenceau wanted Germany crushed. He wanted German territory and money to pay for all the losses suffered.

• Prime Minister Orlando

Italy wanted the promises made to it in 1915 fulfilled. Italy had been promised territory which would be taken from a defeated Austria-Hungary if it left the Triple Alliance and joined the Allies in the war. Orlando was at Versailles to make Italy's claim.

4. The Treaty of Versailles, 1919

During the months of negotiations at which no German delegate was present, it became clear that none of the major peacemakers were going to get their way. The result was a compromise, pleasing no one, least of all the Germans.

The Terms of the Treaty of Versailles

- **Land**
  - *Germany lost Alsace Lorraine to France, West Prussia to Poland, and other areas to Belgium and Denmark.*
  - *Saarland – to be run by the League of Nations*
  - *Danzig – a free city to be run by the League of Nations*
  - *The Rhineland remained German but became demilitarised.*
  - *Germany had to give up its overseas colonies.*
- **Germany's Armed Forces**
  - *The army was to be 100,000 men*
  - *No air force*
  - *Navy to be six battleships only*
- **Reparations**
  - *Germany to pay the Allies £6,600 million for causing the war*
- **War Guilt**
  - *Germany had to accept the blame for causing the war – the War Guilt Clause – Article 231.*

4. The Treaty of Versailles, 1919 (cont.)

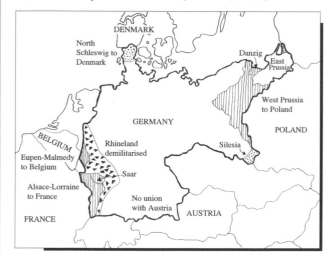

5. Germany's reaction to the Treaty

Germany was angry at the Treaty because:

- it was never consulted about it. The Treaty was a *Diktat* – a dictated peace forced on Germany.

- it hated the shame of the War Guilt clause. It believed other countries had also been to blame for the war.

- it was forced to pay the Allies reparation payments for causing the war.

- it lost its colonies and some of its land which were given to the Allies as war booty.

- it believed that it did not deserve to be punished so severely since the Kaiser and the generals had gone.

In addition,

- the German Navy commanders were angry because they believed that the Navy had not been defeated. Rather than be captured by the Allies, the High Seas Fleet scuttled itself at Scapa Flow.

- the new civilian government was angry because it felt it had little chance of success after the terms had been imposed.

- right-wing groups within Germany were angry with their new government because they thought that it had betrayed Germany by signing the Treaty.

(Later, Germany's unity with Austria was barred, even though self-determination had been given to many other peoples, and this caused further anger.)

As a result, there was a desire for vengeance within Germany.

The search for security – the League of Nations, 1919 – 28

President Wilson aimed to prevent any future international wars. To achieve this, he insisted that all who signed the peace treaties accept his plans for an international organisation designed to maintain peace – a **League of Nations**.

1. Charter of the League of Nations

> ### Charter of the League
> - *To maintain peace by dealing with disputes between countries within the League – by negotiation, not by war.*
> - *To defend the independence of countries and their borders.*
> - *To encourage disarmament.*
> - *To improve the living conditions of all people by tackling problems, e.g. slavery and poor health.*

2. The Covenant of the League

When the League of Nations met in Geneva in January 1920, its aims, rules and methods of working were laid down in the Covenant. This was a series of solemn promises (Articles) not to go to war again which all members agreed to and signed.

3. The Organisation of the League

- ### The Assembly
  Every League member had one vote in the Assembly. The Assembly met once a year.

- ### The Council
  had four permanent members (Britain, France, Italy and Japan) and ten non-permanent members. Major decisions were made by the Council.

- ### The Secretariat
  The League's civil service for record keeping and translations.

- ### Commissions
  were set up to deal with specific problems, e.g. drugs, slavery, refugees, minorities, help for underdeveloped countries, health and mandates for former German colonies.

- ### The Permanent Court of International Justice
  Fifteen judges made decisions on international disputes, if the countries concerned requested the Court to do so.

- ### Agencies
  e.g. The International Labour Organisation.

page learnt

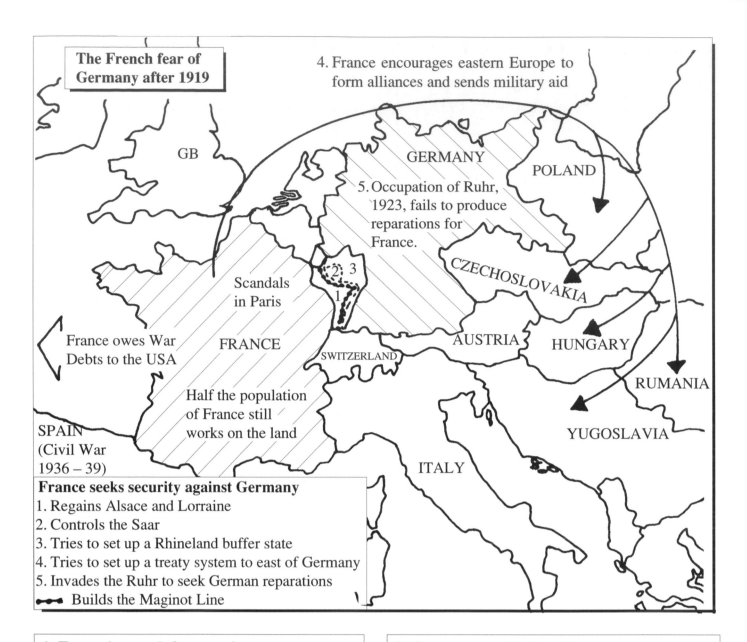

The French fear of Germany after 1919

4. France encourages eastern Europe to form alliances and sends military aid

GB

GERMANY

POLAND

5. Occupation of Ruhr, 1923, fails to produce reparations for France.

CZECHOSLOVAKIA

Scandals in Paris

AUSTRIA

HUNGARY

RUMANIA

France owes War Debts to the USA

FRANCE

SWITZERLAND

YUGOSLAVIA

SPAIN (Civil War 1936 – 39)

Half the population of France still works on the land

ITALY

France seeks security against Germany
1. Regains Alsace and Lorraine
2. Controls the Saar
3. Tries to set up a Rhineland buffer state
4. Tries to set up a treaty system to east of Germany
5. Invades the Ruhr to seek German reparations
■■ Builds the Maginot Line

4. France's search for security

The French were preoccupied in the 1920s with the need for security against future German aggression. France had little faith in the League. This encouraged it to seek allies elsewhere. France made alliances with Belgium in 1920, Poland in 1921, Czechoslovakia in 1924, Rumania in 1926 and Yugoslavia in 1927. France also had its borders guaranteed in 1925 by the **Treaty of Locarno**.

5. German security

Germany was not allowed to join the League of Nations until 1926. Germany remained angry with the Treaty of Versailles. The League was a strong supporter of disarmament, yet only Germany had disarmed. The German people felt isolated because the French made alliances with Germany's neighbours which had large armies.

5. German security (cont.)

• In 1923 French and Belgian troops invaded the Ruhr when Germany failed to make its reparation payments. Britain did not support this action. When this problem was finally resolved in 1924, Germany, under Chancellor Gustav Stresemann, began to have improved relations with the rest of Europe.

• In 1925 Germany accepted its western borders by signing the Treaty of Locarno.

• In 1926 Germany joined the League of Nations.

• In 1928 Germany was one of the 65 countries which signed the **Kellogg-Briand Pact** renouncing war.

Improved relations between France and Germany in the 1920s led to a series of **Disarmament Conferences** in the 1930s. These conferences, however, achieved nothing.

6. International Co-operation and Conflict: 1930s – 1960s

The drift to war, 1933 – 1939

1. German rearmament, 1933 – 39
On 30 January 1933 Adolf Hitler became Chancellor of Germany. He had promised to overthrow the Treaty of Versailles. The rearmament of the German armed forces was his first step in achieving this.

The Road to War	
• *1933*	*Hitler began to rearm secretly as soon as he came to power. Germany failed to secure the disarmament of other countries at the Disarmament Conference or to be treated as an equal power. Hitler walked out.*
• *1933 – 1935*	*Germany trebled its expenditure on rearmament.*
• *1934*	*Germany left the League of Nations.*
• *March 1935*	*Hitler introduced conscription. He declared that Germany would have an army of 500,000 troops.*
• *June 1935*	*Britain and Germany signed the Anglo-German Naval Treaty. This allowed Germany's Navy to be 35% of the strength of the Royal Navy. France was furious: Britain was accepting Germany's right to rearm.*
• *1935 –1938*	*Germany more than doubled its expenditure on rearmament.*
• *1936*	*Hitler allowed his Luftwaffe to fight on the Nationalists' side in the Spanish Civil War.*
• *March 1936*	*Hitler reoccupied the Rhineland.*
• *March 1938*	*Hitler invaded Austria which became part of Germany – Anschluss (= Joining together).*
• *Sept 1939*	*Germany invaded Poland. Britain declared war on Germany.*

2. The effects of German rearmament
- Germany built forts along the Rhine to prevent a possible invasion by Britain and France.
- Germany could protect her industrial might in the Ruhr.
- Germany now had troops along the border with France.
- The smaller powers who had made alliances with France knew that these treaties were of little value.
- Lack of opposition to the Rhineland reoccupation and *Anschluss* made Hitler more daring.

2. The effects of German rearmament (cont.)
- Britain and France were forced to increase their armed forces.
- Since Italy could not trust the British and French to stop German rearmament, in 1935 Mussolini came to terms with Germany. In 1936 Germany and Italy signed the **Rome-Berlin Axis**.
- Once again, Europe was dividing into two opposing camps.

3. The Czech Crisis, 1938
After successfully taking over the Rhineland and Austria without opposition, Hitler set his sights on Czechoslovakia. Three million Germans lived in an area of Czechoslovakia which became known as the Sudetenland. Although this area had never been part of Germany, Hitler wanted it in the Reich. The Czech Nazi Party began to stir up trouble. Hitler was secretly paying them to do this, but stated publicly that he would not allow the Germans in Czechoslovakia to be treated badly. He demanded the area be given to Germany.

The British Prime Minister, Neville Chamberlain, decided to intervene to try to arrange a settlement which would avoid a war. He believed he could make a deal with Hitler.

September 1938
• **15 Sept 1938 – Meeting at Berchtesgaden**
Hitler insisted that the Sudetenland become part of Germany. He agreed to allow time for Britain and France to discuss this. Although France had a treaty with Czechoslovakia, it forced the Czech government to agree to Hitler's demands. It would not help if Czechoslovakia were attacked.
• **22 Sept 1938 – Meeting at Bad Godesberg**
Hitler had changed his mind. He wanted the Sudetenland immediately.
• **29 Sept 1938 – Meeting at Munich**
Hitler agreed to a conference to discuss the problem with Britain, France and Italy. The Czechs were not present. The four powers agreed that:
- German troops should occupy the Sudetenland on 1 October.
- the claims of Poland and Hungary for parts of Czechoslovakia should be accepted.
- Britain and France were to protect what was left of Czechoslovakia.
• **30 Sept 1938 – Munich Agreement**
*Hitler and Chamberlain signed a separate **Munich Agreement** in which the two countries agreed never to go to war with one another.*

4. The end of Czechoslovakia

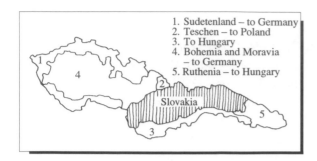

1. Sudetenland – to Germany
2. Teschen – to Poland
3. To Hungary
4. Bohemia and Moravia – to Germany
5. Ruthenia – to Hungary

Czechoslovakia disappeared in March 1939.
- Germany seized the Sudetenland, Bohemia and Moravia.
- Hungary seized Ruthenia and southern Czechoslovakia.
- Poland took Teschen.
- Slovakia declared itself independent.

5. The effects of the Czech Crisis
- Hitler gained Czechoslovakia.
- He believed he could now take Poland without opposition.
- Not yet ready for war, Hitler was given time to prepare.
- Britain and France realised that Hitler could not be trusted.
- France lost its allies in the east who went on to improve their relations with Germany.
- The Soviet Union lost any faith it had in Britain and France.

6. The failure of appeasement
The policy which Neville Chamberlain followed in his dealings with Hitler was called appeasement. Appeasement allows one side, from a position of strength, to negotiate with another and, if necessary, give in to the other's demands if they are justified. Chamberlain wanted to avoid a repetition of the horrors of 1914 – 18; he believed that war could be avoided by satisfying Hitler's demands. War was not avoided – Czechoslovakia was sacrificed and appeasement failed. Hitler got everything he wanted and Britain, France and Italy did little to stop him.

7. The attack on Poland, 1939
The Treaty of Versailles of 1919 *(see pages 26 and 27)* split Germany into two. The Polish Corridor, containing the free city of Danzig, left East Prussia separate from the rest of Germany. Danzig was a German city. Hitler wanted Danzig and the Corridor.

7. The attack on Poland, 1939 (cont.)
Britain and France declared that they would support Poland if it were attacked by Germany. Hitler did not take this seriously. He knew that no British plane could fly as far as Poland. Britain and France tried to come to an arrangement with Joseph Stalin. Hitler, however, knew that their discussions were not going well. Germany was able to attack and defeat Poland, but not the Soviet Union as well. As in 1914, Germany was desperate to avoid a war on two fronts.

8. The Nazi-Soviet Non-Aggression Pact, August 1939

The Nazi-Soviet Non-Aggression Pact, August 1939

Hitler and Stalin signed an agreement not to fight each other. This seemed strange since Nazis hated Communists. Each leader, however, had his own reasons for signing the Pact: Stalin, who felt isolated, bought time, while Hitler had Stalin's pledge that the Soviet Union would not stop his invasion of the Polish Corridor. There was also a secret part to the Pact which prepared the way for Poland to be split between the two countries.

9. War
Germany invaded Poland on 1 September 1939. On 3 September Britain and France declared war on Germany. World War II had begun.

The experience of war, 1939 – 1945

1. The first year of war in Europe
Little fighting took place in 1939. The main losses were at sea: 26 ships were sunk by German U-boats. The 'Phoney War', as it was known, ended in April 1940 when Germany invaded Denmark and Norway. On 10 May 1940, Chamberlain resigned and Winston Churchill became Prime Minister. On the same day, Germany invaded Holland and Belgium. Within a week, the Germans had reached the English Channel. The 250,000 soldiers of the British Expeditionary Force (BEF) and 100,000 French troops were forced to evacuate at Dunkirk. On 22 June 1940 France surrendered.

2. *Blitzkrieg*

means 'lightning war' and describes the tactics used by Hitler to defeat an enemy. Dive bombers of the *Luftwaffe* struck enemy positions. Tanks moved in to destroy them completely, followed by the infantry for any remaining hand-to-hand fighting and to hold the land taken.

3. The Battle of Britain, July – September 1940

• *'Operation Sea Lion'*

Britain was now alone and was next on Hitler's invasion list. His invasion plan was called 'Operation Sea Lion'. In order to defeat Britain, the RAF had to be beaten first. Hermann Göring, the head of the *Luftwaffe*, promised Hitler he could achieve this. He was wrong.

• *The Blitz*

Göring's failure to defeat the RAF resulted in a change in tactics by the Germans. Night raids on British towns and cities plunged Britain into the *Blitz*. Attacks were most intense between the autumn of 1940 and the spring of 1941. 40,000 people were killed and 2 million were made homeless during the *Blitz*.

4. Other major war zones

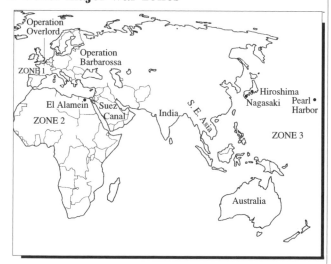

• *The War in Europe (Zone 1)*

With some support from Italy, Hitler controlled most of Europe by 1940. Hitler ordered the start of 'Operation Barbarossa', the invasion of the Soviet Union, on 22 June 1941. Although successful in the summer months, Hitler finally had to abandon the attack in December. He had to be content with the land taken, which the Red Army fought to recapture for the rest of the war. Casualties were enormous.

• *The War in Africa (Zone 2)*

Italy wanted Egypt (ruled by Britain) and the Suez Canal. An attack began in September 1940. Germany supported Italy. In 1942 General Montgomery's forces defeated General Rommel at the Battle of El Alamein. This victory marked the end of hostilities in Africa as a major war zone.

• *The War against Japan (Zone 3)*

The USA did not want to be involved in the War. It had neither signed the Treaty of Versailles nor joined the League of Nations. But American help was given to the Allies – ships, naval bases, arms, money and food. This changed on 7 December 1941 when the Japanese bombed the US naval base at Pearl Harbor. The following day the USA declared war on Japan.

The Japanese captured much of south-east Asia and went on to threaten India and Australia.

5. Victory

• *In Europe (Zone 1)*

- Germany had been beaten in the Soviet Union by 1943.
- Italy was invaded and plans were prepared for an Allied invasion of France. 'Operation Overlord' was the code name given to the Normandy Landings of June 1944. Within a month most of Normandy was in Allied hands. Paris was liberated on 24 August 1944.
- The Germans were surrounded from the south and west by the British and Americans and from the east by the Russians. Germany itself was being bombed from the air. Russian tanks were in Berlin in April 1945.
- Hitler committed suicide on 30 April. On 8 May 1945 Germany surrendered.

• *In Africa (Zone 2)*

Germany had been beaten in Africa by early 1943.

• *Against Japan (Zone 3)*

Japan was alone. However, to invade Japan would cost thousands of lives and might take months. The Allies decided to drop an atomic bomb on a Japanese city to force them into submission. The bomb was dropped on Hiroshima on 6 August 1945. Over 100,000 were killed or injured. When the Japanese refused to surrender, a second atomic bomb was dropped on Nagasaki, killing over 40,000. The Japanese surrendered on 15 August 1945.

page learnt

The experience of war on the Home Front

The war affected almost every aspect of people's lives.

1. Civil Defence

• *Blackouts and other precautions*

Fear of German bombers resulted in the immediate introduction of blackout regulations. When the air raid siren sounded, all street, house, shop and car lights had to be switched off. Dimmed torches and headlights were allowed. Important buildings were surrounded by sandbags. Art treasures and objects in museums were taken to secret locations.

• *Effects*

- Luminous paint became popular.
- Road accidents doubled.
- Pedestrian accidents increased greatly.
- Cat's-eyes were used for the first time.

2. The ARP

The ARP (Air Raid Precautions) was set up in 1937. Volunteers were trained in first aid and watched for fires. Fear of gas canisters being dropped by the enemy persuaded the government to issue everyone with gas masks. They were never needed, however, since gas bombs were never used.

3. Evacuation

To protect children from air raids and gassing, families were encouraged to send children away from large towns and cities into areas less likely to be bombed. For many children the experience was a great adventure; for others it was not. Some children went to Canada and the USA until the U-boat menace made the journey too dangerous.

4. Bomb shelters

The government provided shelters for people with gardens. These corrugated iron structures were called Anderson Shelters and were built into large holes dug in the ground. Families had to go into these whenever the sirens sounded. For those in flats, an iron cage called the Morrison Shelter was designed to fit under the dining table. Most towns and cities had large air raid shelters for those not at home when the bombers came. Thousands spent many nights in London's Underground during the *Blitz*.

5. Shortages and rationing

German U-boats sank many of Britain's merchant ships. This caused great shortages of food and other essential supplies in Britain.

A massive propaganda campaign was started asking people to conserve and grow more food, and avoid waste. The 'Dig for Victory' campaign helped to reduce shortages. In order to give everyone a fair share, rationing was introduced. Sugar, butter, bacon and ham were rationed in January 1940. Other foods followed later. In 1942 the Ministry of Food gave out ten million copies of recipes using unusual ingredients, e.g. omelettes without eggs!

6. Women at war

As in World War, women took over jobs in World War II normally done by men. Factories, shipyards and transport services all employed large numbers of women. Many had specific jobs relating to the war, e.g. in The Women's Land Army. In 1941 women under 50 years old had to register for war work. By 1943 three out of every four women were involved in war work.

7. Conscription

began in April 1939. Young men were called up for periods of six months. When the war started, conscription was extended to all men between 18 and 41 years old.

8. The Home Guard

was set up to protect the country against enemy spies and paratroopers because of the threat of invasion after Dunkirk. It was made up of men who were beyond the age limit for conscription, who had failed the medical inspection or who worked during the day in essential industries. It was affectionately known as 'Dad's Army'.

9. Propaganda and censorship

The government organised various propaganda campaigns on radio, film, newsreel and in newspapers. Posters warned of spies and the black market. Censorship of information was considerable. News of war events abroad was carefully edited. All soldiers' letters were censored before they were sent.

New technology and its effects on the War

1. A war of machinery

More than any previous conflict, World War II was a war of machinery and technology – tanks, aircraft, motorised columns, heavy artillery, ships and submarines. The **superior industrial** and **military strength** of Britain, the Soviet Union and the United States made Allied victory inevitable.

2. Tanks

were able to travel at 20 mph. Their armour made them safe from enemy machine gun fire. An armoured division of tanks with lorries (to carry supplies) could break through enemy lines and therefore attack from the front and the rear. Huge distances could be covered in a day.

3. Aircraft

• *Strategic bombers*

dropped two types of shell – high explosives and incendiary bombs – on factories and civilians.

• *Tactical bombers*

dropped the same two types of shell, but on different targets – troops and warships. Allied bombers dropped 1,275 million tons of bombs on Germany during the war, half of which were dropped on German cities. The only defence against these bombers was to have sufficient fighter aircraft to shoot them down.

• *Long distance aircraft*

sank submarines with depth charges.

• *Spotter aircraft*

worked with warships and protected convoys of merchant ships. Over half of the 750 U-boats sunk during the war were destroyed by aircraft.

4. Ships

Unlike in World War I, some of the most important battles in World War II were fought at sea. World War II was the first war to use aircraft carriers, some of which were capable of carrying over 100 planes. Cruisers, destroyers and battleships were equipped with guns which could fire not only at other ships but also at planes flying overhead.

5. U-boats

German U-boats travelled in 'wolf packs'. Six million tons of Allied shipping were sunk in 1942 and 22 million tons during the whole war.

6. Radar

could locate enemy submarines and provide early warning of aircraft. After further development, radar's electronic eye could measure the exact distance and path of any large object at sea. Radar could be made useless by 'Window' – millions of pieces of silver paper dropped from aircraft. Of all the countries at war, Japan was the slowest to develop radar. Had Japan developed it sooner, the war in the Pacific might have been quite different.

7. ULTRA

The British use of ULTRA was developed further in 1941 to decode German messages. U-boats were now more easily detected.

8. New weapons

• *Bouncing bombs*

Dr Barnes Wallis, a brilliant British engineer, devised a special type of bomb in 1943 to destroy the enormous dams needed for German industry in the Ruhr. These bombs were dropped by Lancaster bombers exactly 60 feet above the surface of the water. They bounced along the surface of the water before hitting the dam wall. They then sank to a point where they exploded like a depth charge.

• *Long-range rockets*

German scientists developed the V-1 and V-2 rockets (flying bombs) in 1944 and 1945. When launched from mainland Europe, they could reach London.

• *Atomic bombs*

These highly destructive bombs were used twice by the USA against Japan.

A United States B29 bomber, the 'Enola Gay', dropped the first atomic bomb on Hiroshima on 6 August 1945. The explosion was equivalent to 20,000 tons of TNT. On 9 August a second bomb was dropped on Nagasaki and as a result Japan surrendered. *(See also page 31.)*

page learnt

Britain, the USA and the USSR after 1945

1. Superpowers

The USA and the USSR had become the two most powerful countries in the world by 1945. The **industrial** and **military strength** of these two countries made them superpowers. Britain's remaining power lay in its Empire.

2. Britain and the break up of its Empire

☒ The British Empire in 1919

• *Importance of the Empire*

The British Empire supplied Britain with an endless source of raw materials and vast markets for its manufactured goods.

• *Independence*

The Empire was beginning to break up, however, even before World War I. Canada, Australia and New Zealand had their own Parliaments.

By 1945, most of the colonies which had fought with Britain felt they should be rewarded with greater independence. The fight for independence had begun in India long before World War II. In 1947 the independent countries of India and Pakistan were created. Many people in Britain were concerned that some colonies were not ready for independence. They felt that instability, and possibly civil war, would break out if British rule came to an end.

• *The Commonwealth*

The British Commonwealth of Nations was created in 1952. Its members were Britain and all Britain's former colonies. Despite the differences in size, populations, wealth and language, all members were considered equal. The Queen remained Head of State.

It was clear after 1945 that Britain's loss of colonies and the effects of the war had reduced its power and position in the world.

3. The USA and Marshall Aid

The USA decided that it was not going to disappear from world affairs in 1945 as it had done in 1919. President Harry S. Truman decided to intervene in Europe to prevent the spread of Communism and the return of Nazism.

General George Marshall was put in charge of sending aid to European countries which had suffered during the war.

Over $13 billion was sent by the USA between 1948 and 1951 to aid Europe's recovery. This money was desperately needed. However, it also helped to divide Europe into East and West because Stalin prevented any of it reaching Communist (Eastern) countries.

4. The USSR and the spread of Communism

The division of Europe after 1945

1 Russian sector of Austria
2 American sector of Austria
3 British sector of Austria
4 French sector of Austria

Stalin believed that the Soviet Union had been easily attacked by Germany because its neighbours – Poland, Rumania, Hungary and Bulgaria – had been unfriendly to the Soviet Union. He did not want this to happen again. Stalin wanted neighbouring countries to have governments friendly to the Soviet Union. In practice this meant setting up Communist regimes in them.

The Americans wanted Czechoslovakia to receive Marshall Aid. Stalin refused to allow this.

Poland, Czechoslovakia, Hungary, Bulgaria, Rumania and Albania all fell under Soviet domination between 1945 and 1948.

Yugoslavia had a Communist government but refused to be dominated by the USSR.

☐ page learnt

5. Germany: East and West

Germany was split into East and West in 1946. West Germany was divided into three sectors controlled by Britain, France and the USA. East Germany was controlled by the USSR. The same system of division was imposed on Berlin.

President Truman made it clear in 1947 that he would oppose any further spread of Communism. This policy was known as the **Truman Doctrine**. The **Cold War** was beginning.

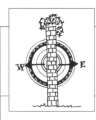

The United Nations, NATO, the Warsaw Pact and the Crises in Berlin and Cuba

1. The United Nations

Representatives from fifty countries met in San Francisco in 1945 to set up the United Nations Organisation (the **UN**). It replaced the old League of Nations. Its main aims were set out in a document called the **Charter**.

• *The General Assembly*
Every member country is represented in the General Assembly and has one vote. Its main function is to make recommendations to other UN bodies.

• *The Security Council*
is the most important body of the UN. It has five permanent members (USA, Russia, Britain, France and China) and ten other members elected from the Assembly for two-year periods. It can impose sanctions and send troops to trouble spots. It cannot, however, interfere in the internal affairs of a country. Every member of the Security Council has the right to **veto** a decision.

• *The Secretariat*
runs the daily administration of the UN from its headquarters in New York. It is led by the Secretary General.

• *The International Court of Justice*
Headquarters in The Hague. Judges appointed from member states sit in judgement over difficult problems brought to them by the UN countries.

1. The United Nations (cont.)
• *UN Special Agencies*
work on specific problems. They are:
- the United Nations Educational, Scientific and Cultural Organisation (UNESCO)
- the International Labour Organisation (ILO)
- the Food and Agricultural Organisation (FAO)
- the International Monetary Fund (IMF)
- the United Nations International Children's Emergency Fund (UNICEF)
- the World Health Organisation (WHO).

In 1945 there were 50 members of the United Nations; by 1970 the membership had increased to 128.

2. NATO and the Warsaw Pact
• *NATO*
The North Atlantic Treaty Organisation (NATO) was set up in 1949 as a military alliance of the major powers of the Western countries. The twelve members pledged to safeguard each others' freedom, which included defending themselves against the Soviet Union.

• *The Warsaw Pact*
The Soviet Union and the other Communist countries responded to NATO by forming the Warsaw Pact in 1955.

It was clear that the two alliances, armed with nuclear weapons, opposed each other and this deepened the Cold War.

3. The Berlin Crises
• *The Berlin Airlift, 1948 - 9*

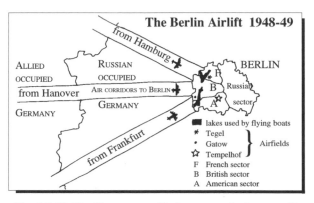

By 1948 Berlin was split into two halves – East and West. The Soviet Union was stripping its half (East Berlin) of all its material wealth. Hundreds of thousands of East Berliners began to move to the West. Stalin ordered that all routes to West Berlin be closed. As Berlin was deep in East Germany, the section controlled by the Allies was cut off.

- *The Berlin Airlift, 1948 – 9 (cont.)*

Stalin wanted to control the whole of the city. He expected Britain, France and the USA would do nothing. He was wrong. The Berlin Airlift began. For eleven months a continuous flow of Allied planes flew into West Berlin, bringing supplies to keep it alive.

Realising the Allies would not give up, Stalin brought the Berlin Blockade to an end on 12 May 1949.

Between 1948 and 1961, 2.6 million people fled from East to West Berlin.

- *The Berlin Wall, 1961*

In 1961 Nikita Khrushchev decided to force the issue of who controlled Berlin once more.
- East Berliners were stopped from crossing to West Berlin to visit relatives or to work.
- Khrushchev sealed the border in August 1961 by building the Berlin Wall.

- *The Berlin Wall, 1961 (cont.)*

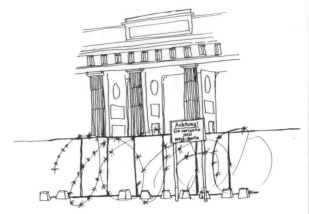

- Trains were stopped. The Underground was blocked off.
- Troops were brought in to stop refugees fleeing.

Berlin became the focus of the Cold War.

4. The Cuban Missile Crisis

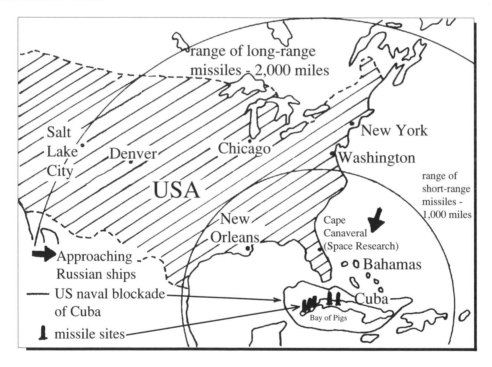

The USA and the Soviet Union came close to war in 1962 when they clashed over Cuba.

In 1959 Cuba had been taken over by a Communist government, led by Fidel Castro. In 1962 the CIA discovered that the Soviet Union had built missile bases on the island aimed at major cities in the USA.

President Kennedy demanded that the missiles be removed. Khrushchev refused. Kennedy then ordered the island to be blockaded by the US Navy. The two nuclear superpowers seemed to be on the brink of war, but in October Khrushchev gave in and ordered the dismantling of the missiles.

page learnt

7. People and Power: Russia 1914 – 1941

The Tsar's Government

1. Autocracy

Tsar Nicholas II, who ruled Russia from 1894 to 1917, was an autocrat: he had complete power. He could pass laws, appoint and dismiss ministers, make international treaties and declare war. There was no Parliament in Russia until 1906. The Tsar had a group of ministers to advise him, but he could ignore their recommendations if he wanted.

To help him rule the country, maintain loyalty and seek out opposition, the Tsar relied on:

- *the Army*
  Its officers were mainly nobles.

- *the Church*
  preached obedience to God and the Tsar.

- *the Nobility*
  kept the peasants under control on their vast estates.

- *the Civil Service*
  maintained existing regime.

- *the Okhrana (Secret Police)*
  found and punished any who were against the Tsar.

2. Inequality

The importance of these groups was not related to their numerical strength. The pie chart below shows the make-up of the Russian population at the end of the 19th century:

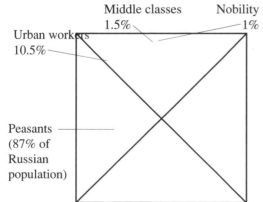

Middle classes 1.5%   Nobility 1%

Urban workers 10.5%

Peasants (87% of Russian population)

80% of the wealth of the country was owned by 2.5% of the population – the nobility and the middle classes, i.e. doctors, lawyers, and merchants.

There were over 100 million peasants.

3. Poverty and discontent

Russia was a backward country in 1914. Its farming methods were out of date and were not able to feed the population. Although Russia was industrialising faster than any other country between 1900 and 1914, it was still far behind most other European countries.

The bulk of the population lived in poverty. Peasants suffered from low wages, long hours, appalling living conditions and the constant threats of disease and death.

After 1900 many peasants left the land to find work in the new factories in the towns and cities. If they were unable to find a shared room in city slums, they were given boxes in factories to live in. They had to work long hours for low wages and lived in foul conditions. Heating, lighting, running water and sanitation were primitive or even non-existent.

All this led to strikes, riots and hatred towards employers.

4. Political opposition

A number of groups and political parties who wished to change Russia began to appear at the end of the 19th century. (Not all, however, were violent revolutionaries, nor did they all meet in secret.)

- *Social Democrats*
  influenced by Karl Marx. They believed in class struggle. They thought that the middle class would overthrow the upper class. This overthrow would then be followed by a revolution of the proletariat (the working class) who would overthrow the middle class. Capitalism would be destroyed. Land and industry would be owned by everyone.

- *Bolsheviks and Mensheviks*
  The Social Democratic Party split in 1903. One group was called the Mensheviks. The Mensheviks were waiting for the right time for a mass revolution supported by all the workers. The other group was the Bolsheviks, led by **Lenin**. The Bolsheviks believed that a small, highly organised party would lead the revolution.

page learnt

4. Political opposition (cont.)

- *Socialist Revolutionaries*
  popular with the peasants. They promised to nationalise all land and industry after a revolution.

- *Cadets*
  made up of middle class conservatives and liberals. They wanted Russia to be more like countries in Western Europe. They did not like the revolutionary attitude of the other parties.

5. Defeats and discontent during World War I

The war was popular at first. Support for the Tsar was strong. However,

- a series of defeats with horrific losses turned the soldiers against the Tsar. The army was badly equipped and poorly trained and led. The soldiers believed that the war was being fought for the benefit of big business and the Tsar.

- Civilians were also suffering. Peasants could not sell their produce as there was no transport. As the peasants made up most of the army, there were few labourers left at home to work on the land. Most horses had been taken for the war. There were terrible food shortages.

- Many nobles and middle class were also displeased with the Tsar's conduct of the war.

The February Revolution, 1917 and the Provisional Government

1. The February Revolution, 1917

The Russian army was close to collapse by the end of 1916.

In February 1917 there were demonstrations in St. Petersburg. Women protested about food shortages. 90,000 people went on strike, with a further 200,000 the following day. Troops who were sent to control them refused to fire and joined the protesters. By the end of the month the Romanov dynasty had ended.

2. Reasons for the abdication of the Tsar

- *The Tsar as commander-in-chief*
  In August 1915 Nicholas became commander-in-chief of the army. The defeats did not stop. He put himself in a position where he could be blamed for Russia's military collapse. The generals wanted him to go.

- *The Tsarina*
  The Empress Alexandra was left in charge of the government while the Tsar was at the Front. She was disliked because she was German. Many felt she was a spy.

- *Rasputin*

  Rasputin was hated for having power over the Royal family, especially the Tsarina. He was very unpopular. Few knew how important Rasputin was in relieving the haemophilia of the Tsar's son, Alexis.

- *The collapse of the government*
  With the Tsar away at the Front and Alexandra unable to cope after the murder of Rasputin, the government in St. Petersburg was in a state of chaos. Food, guns, ammunition and clothing failed to reach the troops.

- *The economy*
  Food shortages and high prices were becoming unbearable. Apart from the endless queues, there were frequent riots and demonstrations.

- *The state of the army*

  Mutinies became more widespread. All ranks became demoralised by their numerous defeats. The troops heard of what was happening at home. Many wanted to go back to their families.

- *The role of the Duma*
  Russia had a *Duma* (Parliament) after 1906. Its powers were limited, however, and it seldom received the support of the Tsar.

  The *Duma* supported the Tsar in 1914, but by 1917 this support had gone. It demanded a change in the government.

3. The Provisional Government

Three days before the Tsar abdicated, the *Duma* set up a committee to take over the running of the government. This self-elected committee became the **Provisional Government**. Its leading member was Alexander Kerensky.

In the same building, a *Soviet* (Council) made up of representatives of soldiers and workers was being created. This was the ***Petrograd Soviet***.

4. Problems facing the Provisional Government

• *The War*

The Provisional Government was committed to continuing and winning the war. This was its biggest mistake and the main reason for opposition to it. When Kerensky became Minister of War, he prepared for a summer attack on the Austrians. He believed that a victory would gain support for the Provisional Government. The Russian army, however, was defeated.

• *The state of the country*

Russia was near to collapse. Mutinies were common, shortages and high prices continued.

• *The return of Lenin*

In April 1917 Lenin returned from exile. Bolshevik support increased during the summer. Although Lenin started out as only one of many revolutionaries, he soon became the most important. When the Provisional Government tried to arrest him in July, he was forced to flee to Finland.

• *The Kornilov Affair*

General Kornilov attempted to take over Petrograd in September 1917 and set up a right-wing dictatorship. Bolshevik leaders were released from prison to help defeat Kornilov's troops. Petrograd workers diverted troop trains. Other troops were persuaded to give up. The ***Bolsheviks*** and the ***Soviets*** – not the Provisional Government – were seen as the saviours of the February Revolution.

By September 1917 the Provisional Government had more enemies than supporters. In addition,
- the social and economic problems had not been solved.
- the war and the defeats were continuing.
- the Petrograd and Moscow *Soviets* commanded greater support.
- the Bolsheviks were preparing to overthrow the Provisional Government.

The Bolshevik Revolution, November 1917

1. Preparing for revolution

By mid-1917 peasants were taking over control of the land. In the cities, conditions were becoming worse. Food, fuel and lighting were in short supply.

The Bolsheviks were preparing for revolution.

- During September the Bolsheviks gained control of the *Soviets*.
- Lenin, in exile, issued instructions to his followers in Petrograd.
- Lenin returned illegally from Finland in the middle of October to take control.
- Trotsky organised the Red Guard of 25,000 troops.
- Trotsky was elected chairman of the Petrograd *Soviet*. He used its Military Revolutionary Committee to organise the revolution.
- The Bolsheviks needed the support of the Petrograd Garrison.

2. The Bolshevik Takeover

The Bolshevik Takeover

- **3 November 1917**
  The MRC gained control of the Petrograd Garrison.
- **5 November 1917**
  Kerensky planned to act against the Bolsheviks by closing down newspapers.
- **6 November 1917**
  Trotsky won the support of the Peter and Paul Fortress garrison. Red Guard captured telephone exchange, power stations, railway stations, banks and bridges.
- **7 November 1917**
  Kerensky left the city to try to get reinforcements. All of Petrograd had been taken except the Winter Palace where the Provisional Government was. 9.40p.m., the cruiser Aurora fired a blank shell at the Winter Palace, as signal for attack. Palace captured without a struggle. Provisional Government surrendered.
- **Later in November 1917**
  Revolutions took place in other cities (including Moscow on 15 November)

3. The Bolshevik Government

Within a week, most of Russia was controlled by the Bolsheviks. There had been little resistance. Lenin knew that he must act quickly to secure his position. He had promised '**Peace, Bread and Land**' to the Russian people.

page learnt

3. The Bolshevik Government (cont.)

• *Treaty of Brest-Litovsk*

Russian
Lands Lost
March 1918

Trotsky concluded a peace treaty with Germany. Russia lost to Germany 33% of its population (62 million), most of its railways, 80% of its coal mines, 25% of its territory and most of its farmland.

• *Elections to the Constituent Assembly*
Lenin decided to let these elections take place on 25 November 1917. When the Bolsheviks won only a quarter of the seats, Lenin said the Assembly was unnecessary. The Red Guards closed it at its first meeting.

• *Decree on land*
Lenin abolished the private ownership of land. All land was now owned by the state.

• *The Congress of Soviets*
The Bolsheviks still had a slim majority in the Congress and on its governing body, the **Presidium**. Lenin used this to control central government. It declared Russia a one-party state. There was no opposition.
The Bolshevik Party was renamed the **Communist Party**.

• *The Cheka*
was set up to deal with public order and crime. It became a powerful police force. It
- dealt with all opposition to the government;
- enforced the strict censorship laws;
- controlled all political activity;
- shot thousands in the Red Terror;
- executed 800 'enemies of the people' after an assassination attempt on Lenin;
- was responsible for the murders of the Tsar and members of his family in July 1918.

• *The Red Army*
Lenin's army for control of the country.

Civil War

1. Reds v Whites
The Civil War was fought from 1917 to 1921 between the Reds (the Bolsheviks) and the Whites (different groups who opposed the Bolsheviks).

The Whites had financial, military and moral support from inside and outside Russia. Outside support came from France, Britain and America. These countries did not want to see a Communist government in Russia. The Whites were expected to defeat the Reds quickly.

2. The White Forces

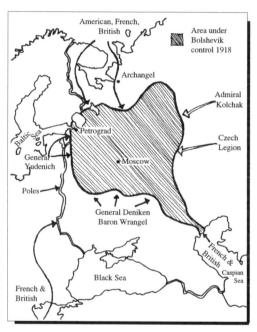

• *The Czech Legion*
These prisoners of war had been refused permission by the Tsar to leave Russia and continued to fight their enemy, Austria-Hungary. When the Communists tried to disarm them, the Legion tried to join up with other White forces. They were prevented from doing so by the Red Army.

• *Admiral Kolchak's Army*
from the east. He wished to set up a military dictatorship with himself as leader.

• *General Deniken's Volunteer Army*
supported the Provisional Government. It was helped by some French and Cossacks. With Baron Wrangel as second in command, they attacked Moscow but failed to take it. This was another victory for the Red Army.

---

page learnt

2. The White Forces (cont.)

- ***General Yudenich's Army***
  from the north. With the help of British tanks, they attacked Petrograd but failed to take it.

- ***The Poles***
  attacked in 1920. They were pushed back to the River Vistula but managed to conclude a peace in 1921. This gave them the land they wanted in the Ukraine.

3. Reasons for the Reds' victory

- ***C**ommanders*
  Trotsky, as Commissar for War, was a brilliant leader of the Red Army. In contrast, the White leaders were lazy, corrupt and brutal.

- ***A**rmies*
  The Red Army was united. In contrast, the White forces never united. The Red Army was also more disciplined than the White forces.

- ***C**ontrol*
  The Red Army kept control of the main lines of communication – the key city of Petrograd and the railways.

- ***A**ims and ideologies*
  The Red Army fought for a single ideology – Communism, while the White forces were divided in their aims.

  (*<u>CACA</u> is another mnemonic to remember – for information about mnemonics, see page 21.*)

4. Effects of the Civil War on the Russian people

The Civil War had dreadful effects on most of the Russian population, especially the peasants.

- When villages were invaded by either side, their loyalty had to be proved.

- If a village had given shelter to one side, it was punished when the opposing army found out.

- Villages were known as White or Red, even if they had no interest in either. If a White village was taken by the Reds (or vice versa), all males would be shot.

- Peasants' crops were burned and livestock stolen or killed to prevent the enemy obtaining supplies.

All this caused starvation and famine on a massive scale.

War Communism

1. State control

Lenin took control of food production and industry to make sure the Red Army had enough food and weapons. This was called War Communism.

> ### War Communism
> - *The State controlled all factories, mines, workshops and railways, including the setting of all targets and wages.*
> - *The State controlled banks.*
> - *No private trading was allowed.*
> - *Grain was taken from peasants.*

2. Reasons for failure

War Communism failed because of

- ***the peasants' non-co-operation***
  Peasants hid their grain and did not supply it to the towns. (If hidden grain was found, the State payment was not made and peasants were imprisoned.)

- ***the 1921 Famine***
  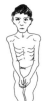 The failure of the harvest in 1921 after three years of civil war caused a terrible famine in which five million people died.

- ***starvation in towns***
  The lack of grain reaching the towns caused starvation. Strict food rationing was introduced. People could only obtain food from the Black Market. (*Cheka* raids failed to stop the Black Market.)

- ***poor industrial output***
  Industrial output did not improve under War Communism.

3. The Kronstadt Revolt

In 1921 sailors at Kronstadt, who had been loyal to the Revolution from the start, revolted. 45,000 troops of the Red Army were sent by Trotsky to crush the rebellion. This was done with great brutality, in one week. Thousands of the sailors were killed during the revolt and thousands more were sent to labour camps.

If even these loyal troops rebelled, then a new policy was needed. Kronstadt finally forced Lenin to change his mind.

---

page learnt ☐

The New Economic Policy

The failure of War Communism led to the introduction of the New Economic Policy (the NEP) in 1921.

The NEP
- *ended the grain seizures.*
- *replaced these with a tax of a fixed percentage of the harvest, paid in grain.*
- *allowed peasants to sell their surplus, so they grew more.*
- *re-introduced private trading – small factories could now be set up.*
- *introduced a new currency.*
- *paid workers in money rather than in goods. The State, however, still controlled all heavy industry – coal, iron, steel, oil, electricity and the railways.*

Many thought Lenin was betraying the Revolution by introducing the NEP. Leading Communists thought Lenin was returning to capitalism.

Stalin

1. Lenin's death
In 1918 Lenin was wounded by an assassin's bullet. Between 1922 and 1923 he suffered three strokes. On 21 January 1924 Lenin died aged 53. Petrograd was renamed Leningrad.

2. Stalin – Lenin's successor
The main rivals for Lenin's position were Trotsky and Stalin. In his *Last Political Testament*, read after his death, Lenin criticised both of them – but particularly Stalin. In 1924 a row broke out between Stalin and the other members of the government. Trotsky wanted International Communism: he believed that the Revolution should be spread to other countries. Stalin followed more closely what Lenin wanted – 'socialism in one country': the revolution should be completed in Russia first. Stalin's point of view was accepted.

Trotsky was removed as Head of the Red Army. By 1927 Stalin had driven Trotsky out of the party. By 1929 Stalin was in charge of the government.

3. Collectivisation
- ### The problem
  By 1929 the government had failed to change Russian farming. Agriculture produced less in 1929 than it did in 1913. There was a desperate need to:
  - produce enough extra food for the towns.
  - sell food abroad in order to buy new machinery from abroad and to pay for foreign experts to come to Russia.

- ### Stalin's answer
  Stalin believed that collective farming was the answer.
  A *kolkhoz* was a collective farm in which all the peasants on the farm shared their private farmland, animals and machinery with each other. Tiny individual farms were cleared to make way for large open fields. The *kolkhoz* was run by a committee of peasants and government farming experts.
  Stalin hoped to collectivise 200,000 villages in the first three months of 1929. Between 1930 and 1934, 50% of farms were collectivised. By 1937 most farms had been collectivised and agricultural output had improved greatly.

4. Setting up a *kolkhoz*
- A group of Communist party members visited a village to plan out the *kolkhoz*.
- *Kulaks* (richer peasants who were against collective farms) had their lands, homes, animals and property confiscated.
- Poor peasants were able to keep their own plots of land or join the *kolkhoz* which had the best land in the village.
- A committee of poor peasants was chosen to work with the party members and farming experts.
- The committee built new houses, food silos, cattle barns, a hospital, a nursery, a schoolhouse and a hen-house.
- The peasants then began to work in gangs.

5. *Kulaks*
Most *kulaks* refused to take part in the *kolkhoz*. They had prospered under the old system. Through hard work they had made their farms profitable. They wanted to keep their profits for themselves. Rather than do what the government said, they killed their horses and cows, hid their grain and refused to plant more. The result was famine: five million *kulaks* died between 1932 and 1934.

6. Industrialisation

In 1930 Stalin stated that Russia was still 100 years behind other industrialised countries. He wanted this difference made up in ten years. This would be achieved by a series of **Five-Year Plans**.

The Five-Year Plans

- *First Five-Year Plan – 1928-32*

  Targets were set for the manufacturing of iron, coal, heavy machinery and chemicals. GOSPLAN, the government's economic planning commission organised the plan. New towns, like Magnitogorsk, were planned. Huge dams to provide hydroelectric power were built. The plan was so successful, according to Stalin, that the targets set were met within four years.

- *Second Five-Year Plan – 1933-38*

  To meet the demands of collectivisation, this plan concentrated on making tractors. Water and transport systems were also improved. By the end of this plan Russia had become the world's third greatest industrial power.

- *Third Five-Year Plan – 1938*

  No priority had been given to consumer goods in the first two plans. This plan was for goods such as radios, bicycles and household goods. However, the threat of war changed this plan. Weapons became the top priority.

By the start of World War II the Soviet Union was second only to the USA in industrial output.

(There is no shortage of statistics produced by GOSPLAN to show how successful Stalin's policies of collectivisation and industrialisation were. Unfortunately most of them are exaggerated and unreliable.)

7. Political Purges

By the early 1930s Stalin's power was immense. He tolerated no challenge to his authority.

- *Kulaks*

  The *kulaks* who resisted his policies of collectivisation were executed in large numbers or transported thousands of miles to work in labour camps. Three million were sent to labour camps in Siberia.

  In 1934 Stalin also decided to eliminate opposition among those closest to him.

- *The murder of Kirov*

  In 1934 a popular leading Communist, Sergei Kirov, was assassinated. It is probable that Stalin planned the assassination himself.

- *The murder of Kirov (cont.)*

  It was the beginning of a systematic purging of all those who had opposed Stalin in the past and those who might do so in the future.

  At first leaders like Kamenev and Zinoviev were expelled from the party. Their imprisonment followed. Trotsky was denounced as the person who had organised all political crimes against the State. Thousands of 'assassins of Kirov' were arrested in the months after the murder and deported.

- *Show trials*

  The first of the infamous show trials was announced on 13 March 1934. Stalin's **Terror** was taking off.

  - Sixteen old Bolsheviks, including Kamenev and Zinoviev, were falsely accused and put on trial. After confessing to crimes they did not commit, they were executed.
  - Thousands more party officials were tried, then shot or deported for similar fictitious crimes against Stalin and the State.
  - 25,000 officers of the Red Army were purged, including the great Marshal Tukhachevsky.
  - Members of the *NKVD* (the Secret Police) who were not good enough at seeking out counter-revolutionaries, or who knew too much about the regime, were purged.
  - Yagoda, the head of the *NKVD*, confessed to fantastic charges under torture and was executed.
  - Wives, parents and children of the accused were considered equally guilty and were also deported to labour camps. Stalin decreed in 1935 that even 12 year olds could be executed.

- *Mass Murder and Labour Camps*

  Most of those who were purged were not tried. They simply disappeared.

  The pace of Stalin's Terror slackened in 1938 (although two million Russians returning from the war in 1945 were sent straight to labour camps). One fifth of the members of the Communist Party were expelled from the Party or shot in the 'Moscow trials'. All rivals, opponents and critics – real or imaginary – were silenced.

  One outstanding critic, however, remained. In 1940 Trotsky was living in Mexico. In August a young Spanish Stalinist broke into Trotsky's house and plunged an ice-axe into his head. Trotsky died in hospital.

  Without question Stalin is one of the greatest mass-murderers in history.

page learnt

8. People and Power: Germany 1918 – 1939

The effects of World War I

1. The end of the War
It was clear by August 1918 that Germany had lost the war. Germany's allies – Austria-Hungary, Bulgaria and Turkey – had surrendered.

2. The mutinies at Kiel and Wilhelmshaven
Sailors at Kiel and Wilhelmshaven mutinied after they had been ordered to attack the Royal Navy. While the soldiers remained loyal, the naval mutiny caused uprisings all over Germany. Workers' and Soldiers' Councils were set up to organise local government. Many felt Germany needed a revolution like the Russian Revolution.

3. The suffering of the German people
Throughout the war, the German people had been told that they were winning the war and that the sacrifices they were making were for the benefit of the army. This was not true.

- With so many men in the army, German food production fell because of the manpower shortage.

- The British naval blockade prevented much needed imports getting into Germany.

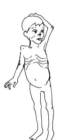

- Food, fuel and clothing were in short supply by 1918, resulting in malnutrition and poverty.

- Rationing was much worse in Germany than in Britain.

- A combination of shortages and Spanish Flu caused the deaths of 400,000 civilians.

4. The fall of the Kaiser
Kaiser Wilhelm II and his generals did not want to make peace.

- They did not want to be held responsible for losing the war.

- They felt that a new civilian government
  - might get better peace terms for Germany and
  - would help the Kaiser to keep his throne.

4. The fall of the Kaiser (cont.)

- They wanted to save the army which would be needed in the future.

Prince Max von Baden became Chancellor. He asked the Allies for peace. President Woodrow Wilson of the USA said that the Kaiser must abdicate first. The Allies blamed him for starting the war and would not deal with him in any peace negotiations *(see page 26)*.

Kaiser Wilhelm II fled to Holland on 9 November 1918. Friedrich Ebert became Chancellor when Germany became a republic after the abdication of the Kaiser.

On 11 November 1918 Germany and the Allies signed an armistice.

5. The Spartacist Revolt
Many towns and cities were run by Workers' and Soldiers' Councils.

On 6 January 1919 the Spartacist League, led by Karl Liebknecht and Rosa Luxemburg, organised an uprising in Berlin.

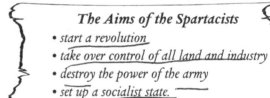

> *The Aims of the Spartacists*
> - *start a revolution*
> - *take over control of all land and industry*
> - *destroy the power of the army*
> - *set up a socialist state.*

Newspaper offices and railway stations were captured. Main streets were barricaded. The rising was defeated in four days by the *Freikorps* – groups of volunteer ex-soldiers who hated Communism. Thousands, including the two leaders, were killed.

6. The Treaty of Versailles, 1919
See pages 26 and 27.

7. Disagreement at Versailles
See page 26.

8. Germany's reaction to the Treaty
See page 27.

The Weimar Republic

1. Elections and the Weimar Constitution

• *Elections*

In January 1919 Germany elected a National Assembly. It met in the city of Weimar. It decided how Germany should be governed.

It elected its first President, Friedrich Ebert, and 600 deputies to the *Reichstag* (Parliament). The leading member of the *Reichstag* was the Chancellor who was chosen by the President.

• *The Weimar Constitution*

> **The Weimar Constitution**
>
> *A number of Fundamental Laws were introduced to protect German citizens.*
> • *No one could be arrested without a trial.*
> • *Police could not enter a person's home without a warrant.*
> • *Freedom of speech and of the press was guaranteed.*
> • *Workers had the right to join trade unions and form political parties.*

2. Economic problems facing the Republic

• *Hyperinflation*

An economic crisis built up between 1919 and 1923. Hyperinflation made the German Mark worthless: in 1919, $1.00 bought 9 Marks; in 1923, it bought 4,200 million Marks.

A new currency, the *Rentenmark*, was introduced in 1923 by the Chancellor, Gustav Stresemann.

• *Reparations*

Germany fell behind in its reparation payments in 1921 *(see page 28)*. France believed Germany could pay if it wanted. Germany missed more payments. French and Belgian troops invaded the Ruhr in January 1923. German workers went on strike – passive resistance. French workers were brought in to replace them.

The Weimar Republic became dependent on foreign money. The 1924 Dawes Plan and the 1929 Young Plan allowed Germany to spread reparation payments over sixty years, reduced the payments by one third and put millions of dollars into the German economy.

2. Economic problems facing the Republic (cont.)

• *The Depression*

This help ended, however, when the Wall Street Crash of 1929 *(see page 46)* plunged Germany into the Depression: almost all American investment in Germany ended; unemployment soared; bankruptcies were common; banks and businesses closed; savings vanished.

The Weimar Republic was blamed for being unable to take Germany out of the Depression.

3. Political weakness of the Republic

• *Proportional Representation*

The system of proportional representation allowed small extremist parties into the *Reichstag* if they received 60,000 votes or more. Some of these parties wished to destroy the Republic.

Also, PR helped to produce coalition governments during the Weimar Republic.

• *Coalition governments*

The coalitions could seldom agree and Germany had 18 coalition governments in the 1920s. This made Germany unstable.

• *Article 48 – Presidential Decree*

In many ways the Weimar Republic was very democratic. However, democracy could be ended at any time by the President who under Article 48 had the power to rule by himself, if he considered it necessary. To place so much power in the hands of one man was dangerous.

4. Political opposition to the Republic

• *Diktat*

The new Republic was hated for signing the Treaty of Versailles. The Treaty was seen by Germans as a *Diktat* – a peace forced on Germany *(see page 27)*.
Some right-wing groups believed Germany had not lost the war. They believed it had been 'stabbed in the back'. Some of these groups wished to overthrow the new government.

• *The Kapp Putsch*

In 1920 Dr Wolfgang Kapp and 5,000 supporters tried to set up a right-wing government in Berlin. The government asked the army to help, but it refused. The revolt was stopped by workers who went on general strike.

page learnt

4. Political opposition to the Republic (cont.)

- **The Munich Putsch**

  Hitler and his *SA* (*Sturm Abteilung*, Storm Troopers or Brownshirts) burst into a beer hall in Munich in November 1923 and announced they were taking over the regional government of Bavaria. They then planned to march on Berlin to set up a new national government. The next day Hitler and 3,000 Nazis marched through the streets of Munich. One hundred police crushed the revolt in which sixteen Nazis were killed. Hitler was sentenced to five years in prison, although he served only 9 months.

The rise of National Socialism

In 1919 Adolf Hitler joined the German Workers' Party. By February 1920 he led the Party and changed its name to the **National Socialist German Workers' Party**.

1. The Nazi Party

Hitler outlined his ideas in his book *Mein Kampf* (*My Struggle*).

The Nazi Party believed in nationalism, racism, strong leadership and struggle.

- **Nationalism**

  The right of all Germans to rule themselves in a Greater German state. *Lebensraum* (living space) for the expanding German population would have to be found in eastern Europe. Hitler intended extending Germany's borders into Poland and eventually Russia.

- **Racism**

  Hitler believed that Germans were Aryans. The Aryans were the 'Master Race'. Hitler believed non-Aryans were inferior races. Jews were not allowed to be German citizens nor to be members of the Party.

- **Strong Leadership**

  The leader of the party was called the *Fuhrer*. His rule was absolute.

- **Struggle**

  Hitler believed that war and conquest were essential for a healthy nation. War and conquest would achieve the goal of *Lebensraum* and prove that Germans were the 'Master Race'.

1. The Nazi Party (cont.)

- **Other features**

  The Nazi Party was also
  - anti-democratic
  - anti-Weimar Republic
  - anti-Versailles
  - anti-Communist
  - anti-Church
  - anti-Jewish
  - anti-trade unions
  - anti-big business.

2. Nazi Party methods

- **Private army**

  Like most new parties in the Weimar Republic, the Nazis had their own private army – the *SA*, led by Ernst Roehm.
  The *SA*'s role was to:
  - protect Nazi speakers
  - collect money for party funds
  - give the party an image of discipline
  - disrupt other parties' meetings
  - smash any opposition.

- **Propaganda**

  was an important factor in the rise of the Nazi party. Under Dr Josef Goebbels:
  - massive campaigns, comprising parades and mass meetings at which Nazi leaders spoke, were held.
  - thousands of posters and slogans were displayed all over German towns and cities.
  - the *Völkischer Beobachter* was the first of many Nazi newspapers to be printed.

3. The rise to power, 1929 – 33

- **The Wall Street Crash**

  In October 1929 the American Stock Market (based in Wall Street, New York) collapsed. Many countries were plunged into an economic depression.

  Germany was hit early and badly. As living and working conditions became worse, the Nazis' policies became more popular.

- **The government's reaction to the Depression**

  The coalition governments were unable to deal with the Depression. They split over policies. New coalitions had to be formed. Many people turned to parties which promised solutions, e.g. the Nazis and the Communists. After 1930 the *Reichstag* was prepared to hand over power to the President and a small group of politicians. Article 48 was used to govern the country.

3. The rise to power, 1929 – 33 (cont.)
• *Election success*

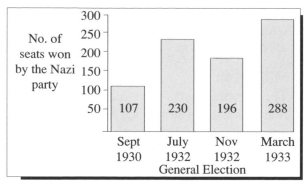

Bar chart: No. of seats won by the Nazi party (vertical axis marked 50, 100, 150, 200, 250, 300)

Sept 1930	July 1932	Nov 1932	March 1933
107	230	196	288

General Election

The Nazi Party achieved great successes in the elections between 1930 and 1933.

• *1930*
107 seats in the General Election

• *1932*
- 13 million people voted for Hitler in the Presidential election against Hindenburg
- 230 seats in the July General Election. The Nazis became the largest party.
- 196 seats in the November General Election. The Nazis remained the largest party.

4. Hitler as Chancellor
Hitler was leader of the largest party in 1933. President Hindenburg did not want him as Chancellor, but knew he must be brought into the government in some way, especially as other leaders were unable to form a government. Hindenburg's group believed that although Hitler was very popular, he could be controlled.

Hitler was finally appointed Chancellor on 30 January 1933, with Franz von Papen as Vice-Chancellor. Only two other Nazis were in the Cabinet.

5. The *Reichstag* Fire
Hitler called an election in March 1933, hoping to get an overall majority. One week before the election, the *Reichstag* building was set on fire. The young Dutchman, Marinus van der Lubbe, who was caught, claimed to be a Communist. Hitler used this as an excuse to seize power.
- He claimed that he had uncovered a Communist plot.
- He obtained from President Hindenburg the special powers given by Article 48.
- He suspended the Fundamental Laws of the Constitution.
- He had 5,000 Communists arrested, including many members of the *Reichstag*.

6. Achieving power
- The Nazis won 288 seats (44% of the votes) in March 1933.
- Hitler's next aim was to secure more power. This was done by passing the **Enabling Law** which allowed him to have laws passed without discussion by the *Reichstag*.
- The Communist Party was banned after the *Reichstag* Fire.
- The Social Democratic Party (SPD) which had 120 seats was banned in June 1933. Other parties dissolved themselves.
- Other members of the Cabinet (except von Papen) were replaced by Nazis.
- In July 1933 the Nazi Party was declared to be the only lawful political party in Germany.

Hitler was well along the road to dictatorship.

Conditions in Nazi Germany

1. The Jews
Hatred of the Jews is called **anti-semitism**. Anti-semitism was not new in Germany. Many countries, including Germany, had been guilty of it for centuries. Hitler claimed that Jews were the cause of all of Germany's problems. Hitler believed that
- the Jews plotted with others during World War I which helped to cause Germany's defeat in 1918;
- Jews plotted with Communists;
- Jewish greed and financial power were ruining Germany;
- Jews, either by themselves or with others, were responsible for everything that was wrong in Germany;
- as long as Jews lived in Germany, the 'Master Race' was contaminated.

The Nazis passed a series of laws against Jews.

Anti-Jewish Laws
From 1933
- *Jewish doctors, lawyers and civil servants were dismissed from their jobs.*
- *Jewish shops were boycotted in April 1933.*
- *Marriage between Jews and non-Jews was forbidden.*
- *Jews were not citizens of Germany, therefore had no vote and no rights.*
- *Jews had to wear yellow stars at all times.*
- *All Jews were given the name Sara or Israel.*

page learnt

2. *Kristallnacht*, 1938.

After a young Jew murdered a German in Paris, a massive anti-semitic campaign, called *Kristallnacht*, began in Germany in which Jewish shops, homes and synagogues were destroyed. 20,000 Jews were arrested and sent to concentration camps.

3. Youth Movements

Hitler was particularly keen to have the young involved in his new Germany. Boys were to be strong and fit to defend Germany; girls were to become the mothers of the 'Master Race'.

Organisations were set up for training boys and girls. Joining them was made compulsory in 1939.

Age (Years)	Boys	Girls
6 to 10	Little Fellows – *Pimpfen*	At home with their mothers
10 to 14	Young Folk – *Jungvolk*	Young Girls' League
14 to 18	Hitler Youth – *Hitler Jugend*	League of German Maidens

Although sinister, the Hitler Youth organisations were popular. Outdoor sports, camping weekends, uniforms, parades, singing, games and competitions were very appealing, especially as most children were involved.

4. Education

 Hitler knew how important it was to control the minds of children.
 • Teachers had to be members of the National Socialist Teachers' League.
• The *Heil Hitler!* salute had to be given in all schools when greeting anyone.
• Nazi songs were sung and Nazi symbols hung in all schools.
• Many courses were rewritten to include Germany's greatness, the 'Master Race' ideology and anti-semitism.

5. Intimidation

Threats and coercion were common in Nazi Germany.
• The Nazi Party disliked trade unions. Trade union leaders were removed. Working men's clubs were closed. Workers were forced to join the *DAF*, the German Workers' Front.
• From 1936 young people who were not members of the Hitler Youth received letters asking them to explain why they were not.
• Teachers who did not follow Party instructions in their lessons were dismissed or imprisoned.
• Church ministers who did not encourage their congregations to support the government were removed and had their churches closed down.

5. Intimidation (cont.)

• The *SA* (disbanded in 1939), the *SS* (*Schutz Staffeln*) and the *Gestapo* (Secret Police) commanded by Heinrich Himmler organised all intimidation in Germany.

6. Militarism

The parades, mass rallies, demonstrations and marches did not stop when Hitler came to power. Discipline was central to Nazi ideology. A military way of life was essential if Germany was to become strong again. The whole population existed only for the greater glory of Germany.
Hitler planned for a war which would overthrow the Treaty of Versailles.

Year	Size of German Army
1919	100,000 men
1936	550,000 men
1938	850,000 men (plus 900,000 reservists)

Hitler spent 73,000 million Reichsmarks on the army, navy and air force between 1933 and 1939.

7. Opposition to the Nazi Regime

• *Socialists and Communists*
Socialists and Communists had been Hitler's greatest opponents before 1933. After the *Reichstag* Fire, many had been imprisoned. Those who remained free set up anti-Nazi groups. Their secret headquarters were frequently raided by the *SA, SS* and *Gestapo*. Although the greatest opposition came from the working class, on the whole they supported the regime.

• *The Christian Churches*
Hitler's attack on religion was slower in being launched. He made a pact in 1933 with the Roman Catholic Church, upholding its rights. Hitler appointed a Protestant minister as Bishop of the Reich to make sure he always received the co-operation of the Protestant Church.
When church ministers hinted at opposition, they were arrested. Pastor Niemöller was imprisoned in 1937 and between 1938 and 1945 he was imprisoned in a concentration camp.
Opposition to Hitler came from individuals within the churches, not from most of their governing bodies. Although there were some individual exceptions, the churches turned a blind eye to the atrocities taking place.